Mobile Design Pattern Gallery

Theresa Neil

O'REILLY®

Beijing · Cambridge · Farnham · Köln · Sebastopol · Tokyo

Mobile Design Pattern Gallery
by Theresa Neil

Published by O'Reilly Media, Inc., 1005 Gravenstein Highway North, Sebastopol, CA 95472.

O'Reilly books may be purchased for educational, business, or sales promotional use. Online editions are also available for most titles (*http://my.safaribooksonline.com*). For more information, contact our corporate/institutional sales department: (800) 998-9938 or *corporate@oreilly.com*.

Editor: Mary Treseler
Production Editor: Dan Fauxsmith
Proofreader: O'Reilly Publishing Services

Cover Designer: Karen Montgomery
Interior Designer: David Futato
Illustrators: Robert Romano and Aaron Jasinski

March 2012:   First Edition.

Revision History for the First Edition:
2012-03-01   First release
2012-04-27   Second release
See *http://oreilly.com/catalog/errata.csp?isbn=9781449336448* for release details.

ISBN: 978-1-449-33644-8

[TI]

1335899687

Table of Contents

Foreword

To name something is to begin to understand it.

My five-year-old son, like many children, enjoys looking at clouds. A few weeks ago, he clued into the fact that different kinds of clouds had different names. And so, being of good geek stock, he proceeded to memorize them—cirrus, cumulus, stratus, cirrostratus, cumulonimbus, altostratus, lenticular; all of the ones I knew, and then some. I'd certainly never heard of "cumulus congestus" before.

Now, when he looks at the sky, he can tell me which clouds are which. More than that, he notices more than he did before, and with greater nuance. He has learned to visually discriminate among cloud types based on texture, color, height, movement, and who knows what else. (They're not always easy to tell apart, of course, but that doesn't bother him.) He can predict, with some accuracy, which ones might drop rain on us and which won't.

And in his limited preschooler's fashion, he uses his cloud knowledge to analyze the big picture. "Cirrostratus clouds might mean a warm front," he points out. Or, "Cumulus congestus might turn into cumulonimbus! Then we could get a storm."

Above all, he enjoys knowing these names. Little kids seem to get a kick out of naming the things they love, whether they're clouds, dinosaurs, bugs, cars, dolls, or movie characters. Certainly their imaginations aren't limited by that left-brain knowledge, despite our grownup romantic biases—my son still sees palaces and ducks and cauliflowers in the clouds, even as he names them "cumulus."

So it is with us grownups. That brings us to the topic at hand: by recognizing and naming patterns in interfaces, we "see" those interfaces better. We notice more details, because our brains are more attuned to what we should look for. We can start to predict the workings of the software we use, because we know how certain interface patterns should behave. Then we can tell other people what we see via an expressive new vocabulary.

And how do we learn these patterns?

When my son learned about clouds, the best tool he had were pictures. Lots of pictures. After looking at some of these "catalogs" in books and websites, he learned to see rather subtle differences between cloud types, some of which are hard to describe verbally.

Likewise, the best way to learn interface patterns is to see visual examples. Now, I'm a writer, so I love words. When not restrained by courtesy, I would happily go on endlessly about what patterns are, how to choose them, and the differences between them! But it's clear to me that anyone who simply wants to design interfaces—that is, anyone who needs to know patterns as one component of their craft knowledge—won't really need all those words. For a given pattern, they need just enough explanation to "get it," and then they need to see a range of well-chosen real life examples to solidify and internalize that knowledge.

In this book, Theresa Neil has pulled together a spectacular collection of pictures of patterns. I can't imagine the work that went into this, having tried it myself—it's no small feat to review this many mobile apps, see what works best in them, and gather up all these carefully catalogued screenshots.

For mobile interface designers, this book is a treasure. Read it straight through if you'd like, but more than that, use its examples to improve your own designs.

- Use your own judgment about what works well in these examples, and figure out what may work best in the context of whatever you're designing.
- Use it as a sourcebook for design inspiration. I found myself admiring these screenshots for design aspects that had nothing to do with the patterns themselves, such as icon design and color usage.
- Use it to expand your knowledge of how existing apps work, without laboriously downloading and using them all (and on several devices, don't forget).

You might even go out and find your own pattern examples in the mobile apps you use daily. In fact, I'd bet that once you learn these pattern names, you won't be able to avoid doing so. Having had my son point out "cumulus congestus" in the wild a few times, I know it well, and, gosh—I don't know how I ever lived without that knowledge.

Enjoy!

—Jenifer Tidwell

Preface

Introduction

We recently had a new mobile project starting and all of our experienced mobile designers were booked. This gave me less than a week to impart my mobile experiences to a new designer. So I made a quick tutorial with lots and lots of screenshots, illustrating good design and not so good design. Gradually a set of patterns for mobile application design emerged.

Even as I was cataloging these patterns, I knew that the real value wasn't only the pattern identification, but in the hundreds of examples I'd captured. So instead of a tome of abstract patterns only an author can love, this book is a showcase, or gallery, of mobile application design. This book includes 400+ current screenshots from iOS, Android, BlackBerry, WebOS, Symbian and Windows applications, organized by pattern type. And the accompanying site: www.mobiledesignpatterngallery (*http://www.mobilede signpatterngallery*), and Flickr photostream have even more examples.

Intended Audience for This Book

The Mobile Design Pattern Gallery is for product managers, designers and developers who are creating mobile applications. As companies are defining and refining their mobile strategy, it can be a challenge to find examples of design best practices, especially for multiple operating systems. Whether you have been tasked with designing a simple iPhone application, or designing for every popular operating system on the market, these patterns will provide solutions to common design challenges.

Safari® Books Online

 Safari Books Online is an on-demand digital library that lets you easily search over 7,500 technology and creative reference books and videos to find the answers you need quickly.

With a subscription, you can read any page and watch any video from our library online. Read books on your cell phone and mobile devices. Access new titles before they are available for print, and get exclusive access to manuscripts in development and post feedback for the authors. Copy and paste code samples, organize your favorites, download chapters, bookmark key sections, create notes, print out pages, and benefit from tons of other time-saving features.

O'Reilly Media has uploaded this book to the Safari Books Online service. To have full digital access to this book and others on similar topics from O'Reilly and other publishers, sign up for free at *http://my.safaribooksonline.com*.

How to Contact Us

Please address comments and questions concerning this book to the publisher:

O'Reilly Media, Inc.
1005 Gravenstein Highway North
Sebastopol, CA 95472
800-998-9938 (in the United States or Canada)
707-829-0515 (international or local)
707-829-0104 (fax)

We have a web page for this book, where we list errata, examples, and any additional information. You can access this page at:

http://www.oreilly.com/catalog/9781449314323

To comment or ask technical questions about this book, send email to:

bookquestions@oreilly.com

For more information about our books, courses, conferences, and news, see our website at *http://www.oreilly.com*.

Find us on Facebook: *http://facebook.com/oreilly*

Follow us on Twitter: *http://twitter.com/oreillymedia*

Watch us on YouTube: *http://www.youtube.com/oreillymedia*

Acknowledgments

Many thanks to my illustrator Aaron Jasinski for designing all the patterns, Chad at Smith & Robot for the Mobile Design Pattern Gallery website and blog design, Mary and Dan at O'Reilly Media for pulling it all together. I also have to thank my talented team, Jessica, James, Kirsten, Marie, Ben, Lulu, Ivan and Enrico for holding the business together the last six months. And my patient family for letting me write every weekend. Special thanks to Jenifer Tidwell and her son Matthew for the wonderful foreword—I hope my readers will enjoy this gallery half as much as an afternoon of cloud watching.

Navigation

Primary Navigation Patterns: Springboard, List Menu, Tab Menu, Gallery, Dashboard, Metaphor, Mega Menu

Secondary Navigation Patterns: PageCarousel, Image Carousel, Expanding List

I like to read reviews in mobile marketplaces to better understand how people are using the apps. The marketplace rating system is an incredibly valuable feedback tool that doesn't exist for web and desktop applications. It provides a rich source of information about customers' preferences and expectations.

In general, most 4 and 5 star reviews aren't very specific. They often sound a lot like this: "What a great app, it looks good and works well". The 1 and 2 star reviews are much more telling; they extensively outline the problems with the application. The most common complaints seem to revolve around:

- Crashing

- Lack of key features (syncing, filtering, account linking…)
- Poor navigation (can't go back, can't find things…)
- Confusing interface design

The first two issues can't be fixed with design patterns, but the third and fourth most common complaints can be. Following common design patterns for navigation will ensure that people can find and use the valuable features in your application.

Primary Navigation Patterns

Good navigation, like good design, is invisible. Applications with good navigation just feel intuitive and make it easy to accomplish any task, from browsing friends to applying for a car loan. While there may be many options for navigating content within an app, I want to focus on seven patterns for primary navigation, i.e., patterns for the main menu:

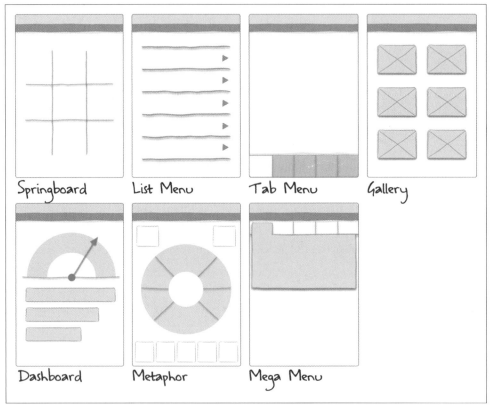

Figure 1-1. Primary Navigation Patterns

Springboard

The Springboard pattern is OS neutral, working equally well across devices. It is also sometimes referred to as a Launchpad. The Springboard is characterized by a landing page of menu options that act as a jumping off point into the application. Facebook followed the Springboard design of the iOS home screen, and they were quickly emulated by other applications.

Figure 1-2. Facebook Springboard and Ovi Maps

Figure 1-3. Trulia and LinkedIn

Figure 1-4. NewsRoom on Palm and Yahoo! on Nokia

Personalized Springboards can be used to display personal profile information inline with the menu options. Typically a customization feature is available for changing the Springboard layout.

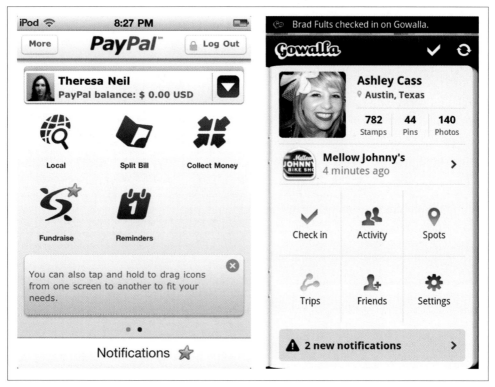

Figure 1-5. PayPal personalized springboard and early Gowalla

Grids for 3x3, 2x3, 2x2, and 1x2 are the most common layouts. But a Springboard doesn't have to follow a grid layout. Some options can be proportionately larger to convey greater importance, like the video option in the Masters iPhone app is two to three times larger than the other menu items.

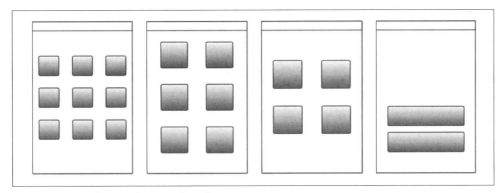

Figure 1-6. Grid layouts for springboards

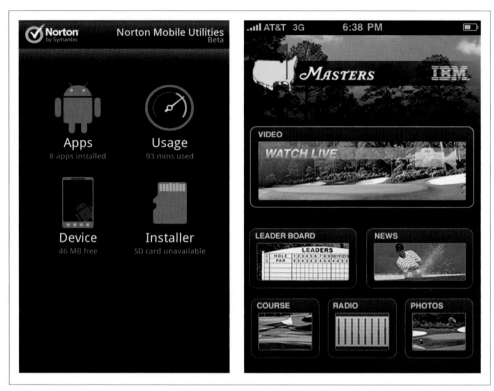

Figure 1-7. 2x2 grid layout, Norton Mobile; irregular layout, Masters

 Use a grid layout for items of equal importance, or an irregular layout to emphasize some items more than others. Consider personalization and customization options.

List Menu

The List Menu is similar to that Springboard in that each is a jumping off point into the application. There are numerous variations of this pattern including personalized list menus, grouped lists, and enhanced lists. Enhanced lists are simple List Menus with additional features for searching, browsing or filtering.

Figure 1-8. List menus: Valspar Paint and Kayak

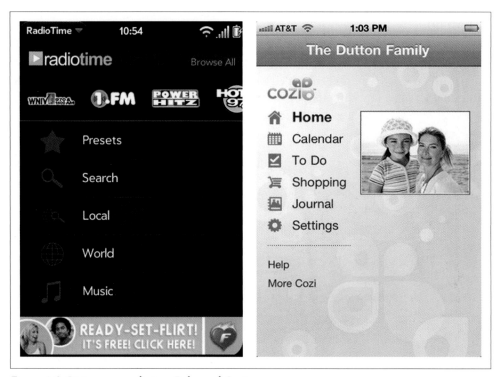

Figure 1-9. List menus: radiotime Palm and Cozi

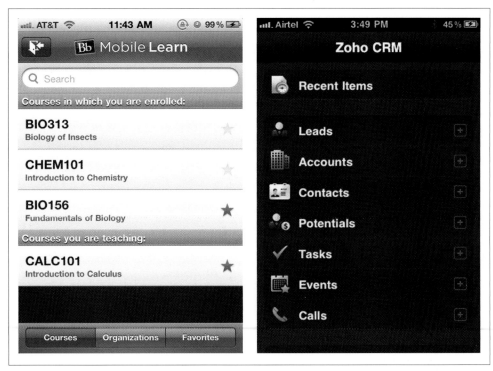

Figure 1-10. Personalized lists: Blackboard and Zoho CRM

Figure 1-11. Enhanced list, Amazon MP3; grouped list, Stratus

 List Menus work well for long titles or those that require sub text. Applications using List Menus should offer an option on all internal screens for returning to the List Menu, usually a button in the title bar with a list icon or the word "menu."

Tabs

Tab navigation is not OS neutral since each OS has their own guidelines for tab location and design. When choosing this pattern for your application, be prepared to customize the tab location for the different OSs.

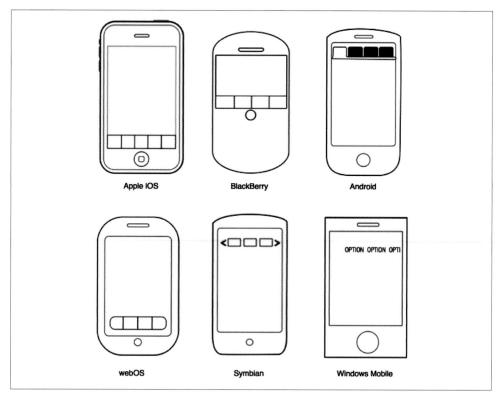

Figure 1-12. Tab orientation for various OSs

Bottom tabs, favored by iOS, WebOS, and BlackBerry, are the most thumb friendly option.

Figure 1-13. Jamie Oliver Recipes and Molome, bottom tabs

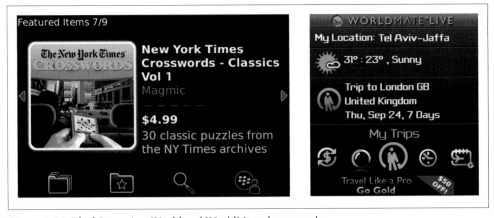

Figure 1-14. BlackBerry App World and WorldMate, bottom tabs

Horizontally scrolling bottom tabs, as shown in the Starbucks and Blue Mobile apps, provide a useful mechanism for offering more options without having to open up a More...screen.

Figure 1-15. Starbucks and Blue Mobile, scrolling bottom tabs

Top tabs, favored by Android, Symbian, and Windows, look familiar since they are modeled after standard website navigation patterns. Nokia and Windows both use scrolling top tabs that you can flick to reveal more menu options.

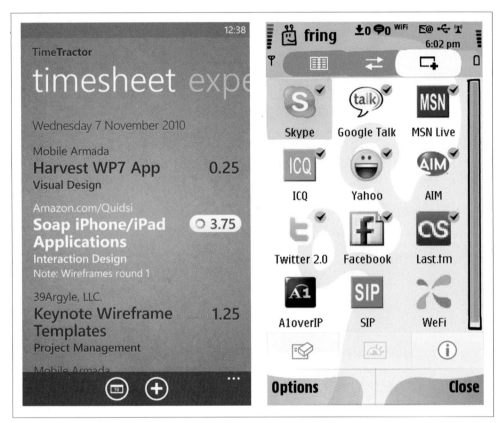

Figure 1-16. Harvest TimeTractor and Fring on Nokia, scrolling top tabs

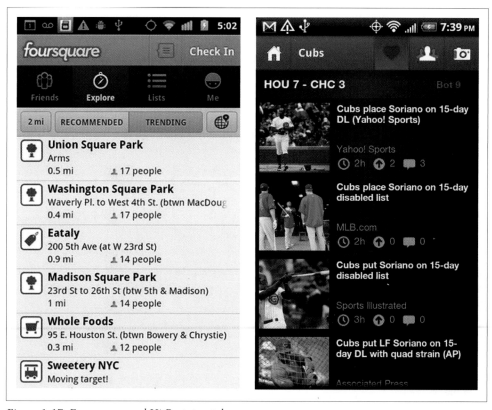

Figure 1-17. Foursquare and HitPost, top tabs

 Clearly indicate the selected menu item by visually differentiating the selected tab from the others. Use easy to recognize icons or icons with labels.

Gallery

The Gallery pattern surfaces individual pieces of content for navigation. Content is usually individual articles, recipes, photos, or products and can be arranged in a carousel, grid, or slideshow.

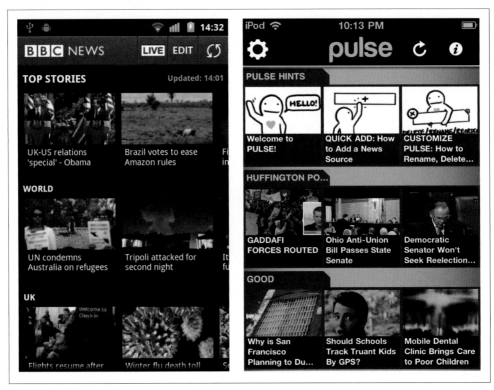

Figure 1-18. BBC and PULSE

Figure 1-19. Flickr and PictureIt Palm

Sometimes the content will be easier to browse if it is grouped. Dwell use side tabs to organize gallery content into manageable chunks.

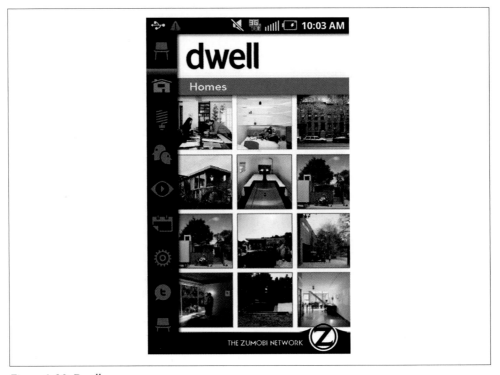

Figure 1-20. Dwell

 The Gallery pattern works best for frequently updated content that people want to browse.

Dashboard

Dashboards provide a roll-up of key performance indicators, KPIs. Each metric can be drilled into for additional information. This primary navigation pattern is useful for financial applications, analytics tools and sales and marketing applications.

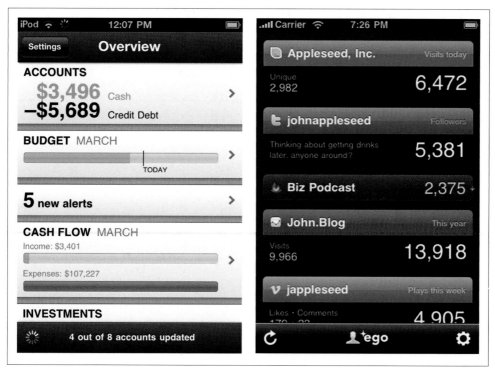

Figure 1-21. Mint and ego dashoards

 Don't overload the dashboard; conduct research to determine the key metrics to include.

Metaphor

This pattern is characterized by a landing page modeled to reflect the application's metaphor. This is used primarily in games, but can also be seen in applications that help people catalog and categorize items, like notes, books, wine, etc.

Figure 1-22. Awesome Note

Figure 1-23. Cellar

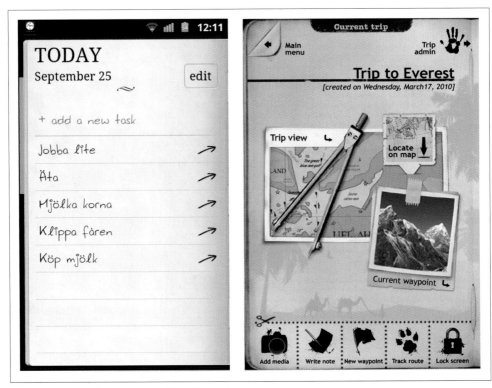

Figure 1-24. DoItTomorrow and TripJournal

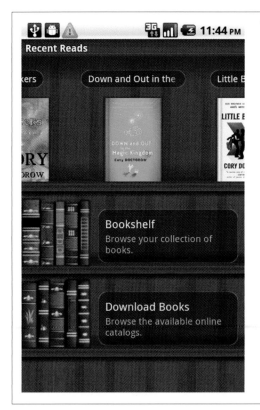

Chapter 1

My girlfriend was 15 percent of my age, and I was old-fashioned enough that it bugged me. Her name was Lil, and she was second-generation Disney World, her parents being among the original ad-hocracy that took over the management of Liberty Square and Tom Sawyer Island. She was, quite literally, raised in Walt Disney World and it showed.

It showed. She was neat and efficient in her every little thing, from her shining red hair to her careful accounting of each gear and cog in the animatronics that were in her charge. Her folks were in canopic jars in Kissimmee, deadheading for a few centuries.

Figure 1-25. Aldiko Book Reader

 Use the Metaphor pattern judiciously, as a poorly implemented meta-phor can look a lot like the Novel Notion anti-pattern in Chapter 10.

Mega Menu

A mobile Mega Menu is like the web Mega Menu, a big overlay panel with custom formatting and grouping of the menu options. The RipCurl website uses a mega menu for navigating into sub categories of clothing.

Figure 1-26. RipCurlShop.com

The webOS version of Facebook uses a megamenu for streamlined navigation, avoiding the extra navigation found in a Springboard pattern. Walmart uses this same pattern in their Android app.

Figure 1-27. Facebook webOS and Walmart Android

 Determine your information architecture before choosing the navigation pattern. Choose a more appropriate pattern, like Tabs, if there are only a few major sections in the app.

Secondary Navigation

This chapter didn't feel complete with only menu patterns, so I broadened it to include secondary navigation. By secondary navigation, I mean the navigation within a page or module. For example, the Springboard in the ANZ application is secondary to the primary Tab navigation. Similarly in Jamie Oliver's Recipes, the List is secondary to the primary Tab navigation.

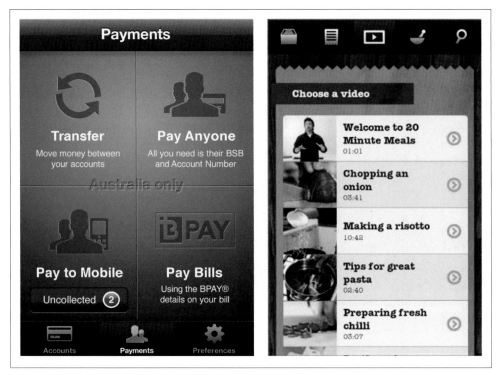

Figure 1-28. (Left) Primary, tabs; secondary, springboard. (Right) Primary, tabs; secondary, list.

Any of the primary navigation patterns can be reused as secondary navigation patterns. It is common to see Tabs with Tabs, Tabs with Lists, Tabs and Dashboard, Springboard and Gallery, etc.

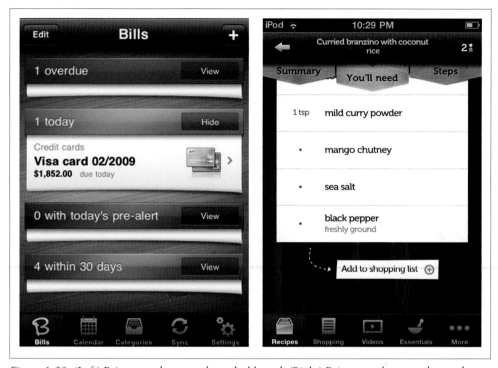

Figure 1-29. (Left) Primary, tabs; secondary, dashboard. (Right) Primary, tabs; secondary, tabs.

There are some additional patterns that work well for secondary navigation, but probably aren't ideal for primary navigation:

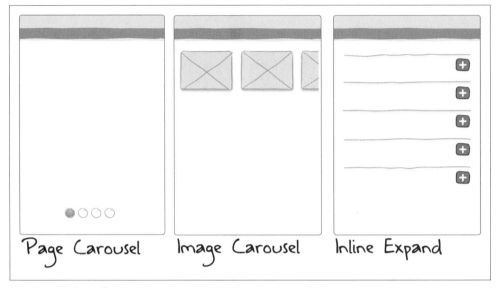

Figure 1-30. Secondary navigations patterns

Page Carousel

This pattern can be used to quickly navigate a discreet set of pages using the flick gesture. The page indicator (the iOS term for the little dots) displays how many pages are in the carousel; flicking displays the next page. All four examples below use the page carousel within a selected tab.

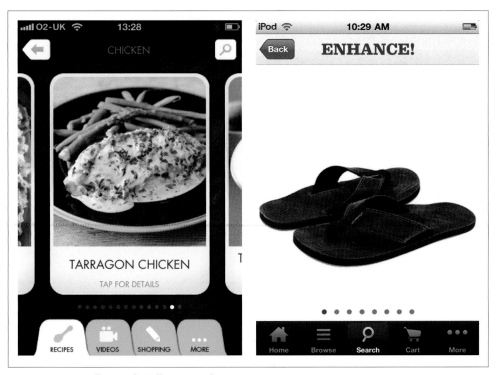

Figure 1-31. Nigella Quick Collection and Zappos

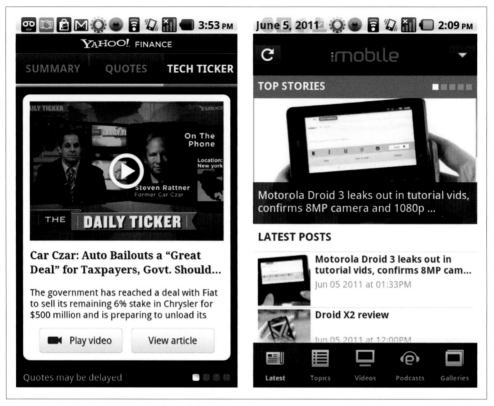

Figure 1-32. Yahoo! Finance and iMobile

The page carousel pattern has its limits. Consider using a list for navigating more than eight pages.

Figure 1-33. ExcellentAnalytics—Too many pages

 The page carousel works best for navigating a small number of pages. Use a visual indicator to reflect the number of screens, and current screen. Flick is the common gesture to navigate the carousel.

Image Carousel

The image carousel may be a 2D carousel or more like the iTunes coverflow. IMDB uses the image carousel to surface the most viewed movies. We used it to display featured products in the retail application we designed for the Adobe Flex Showcase.

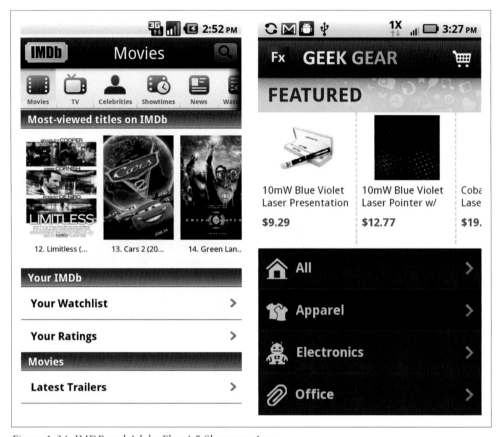

Figure 1-34. IMDB and Adobe Flex 4.5 Showcase App

The Photo Cookbook is another example of the Image Carousel; however, the images are grouped in columns by recipe type.

Figure 1-35. The Photo Cookbook

Tap'n'Scrap has good examples of both styles. They use a 2D carousel for background and frame selection, and the coverflow style scrapbook viewing.

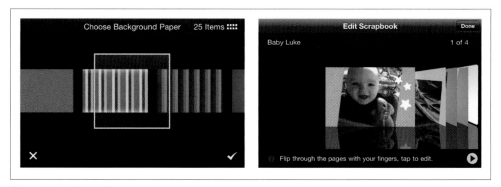

Figure 1-36. Tap'n'Scrap

ANZ's banking app displays account information payment sources in a coverflow. While this is attractive and probably demos well, the excitement of flicking through cards to make a payment probably wears thin after the first few uses.

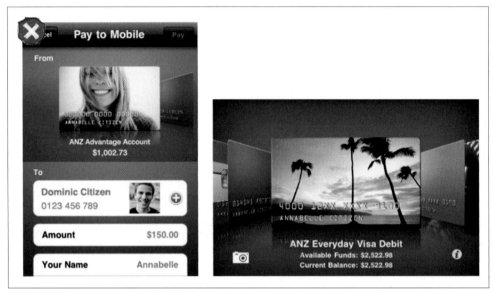

Figure 1-37. Image Carousel in ANZ for payment selection demos well, but gets old fast

 The Image Carousel works best for displaying fresh visual content, like articles, products, and photos. Provide visual affordance, either with arrows, partial images or page indicators (dots) that more content can be accessed.

Expanding List

The Expanding List allows a single screen drill down to reveal more information. Android Gingerbread uses this pattern in the call log. All calls from the same number are collapsed into one row. Tapping the icon expands the list to show the individual instances.

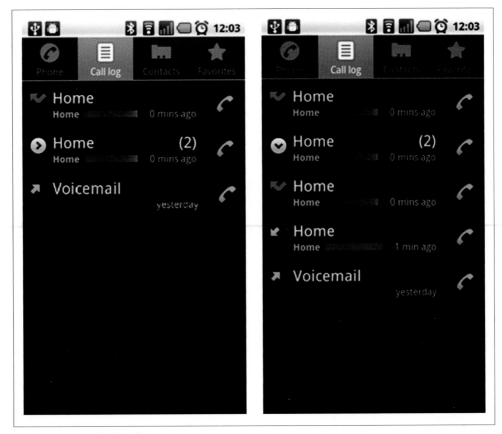

Figure 1-38. Android Call Log

This pattern is more common in mobile optimized websites than mobile applications, but can work well in both cases. Take for example the Gap.com mobile site. The Expanding List is used instead of a Cascading List to disclose all of the Women's clothing categories.

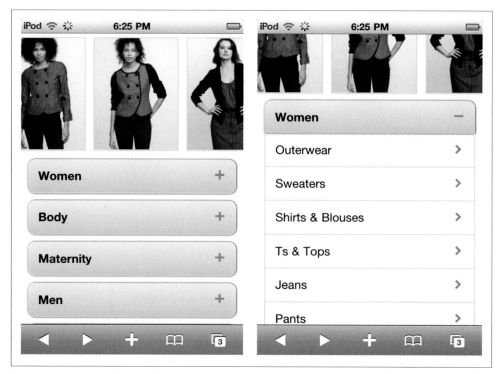

Figure 1-39. Gap Mobile Website

 The Expanding List pattern works best for progressively disclosing more details or options for an object.

CHAPTER 2
Forms

Patterns: Sign In, Registration, Checkout, Calculate, Search Criteria, Multi-step, Long Form

Most web applications rely extensively on forms for data entry and configuration. And although we have compelling research and design strategies for basic form design, there are still horrible forms all over the Web. Since there is usually no alternative, we muddle through them to buy merchandise, submit applications, or answer surveys.

Figure 2-1. Many distinct visual elements on this form get in the way of seeing the questions the form is asking. Wroblewski, Luke. 2008. Web Form Design: Filling In the Blanks. New York: Rosenfeld Media.

Mobile forms, with reduced screen size and restricted input devices, have even less leeway for bad design. Before designing any forms, I highly recommend brushing up on the basics with:

Filling in the Blanks: Web Form Design, by Luke Wroblewski(Rosenthal Media)

Forms on Mobile Devices: Modern Solutions, by Luke Wroblewski(Smashing Magazine)

Mobile Form Design Strategies, by Chui Chui Tan (UX Booth)

The following form design patterns can supplement the information in these books and articles:

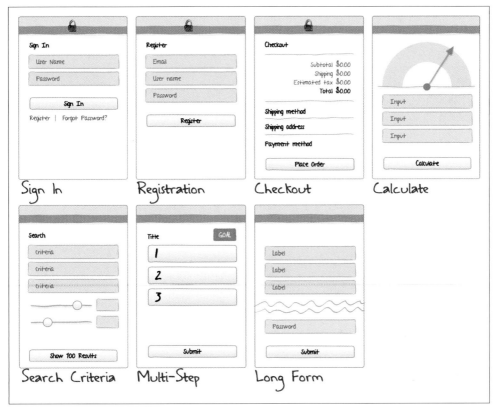

Figure 2-2. Form patterns

Sign In

Sign In forms should have a minimal amount of inputs: user name, password, action button, password help, option to register. Some applications do this in a single screen, like Photobucket and Groupon.

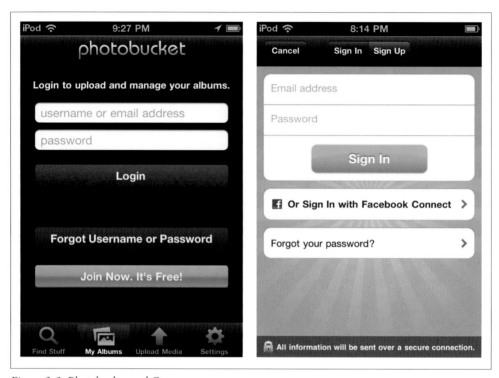

Figure 2-3. Photobucket and Groupon

Other apps, like kik and springpad, present the option to Sign In or Register up front, then take the user to the appropriate form. Springpad and Groupon also offer the option to sign on with Facebook or other services.

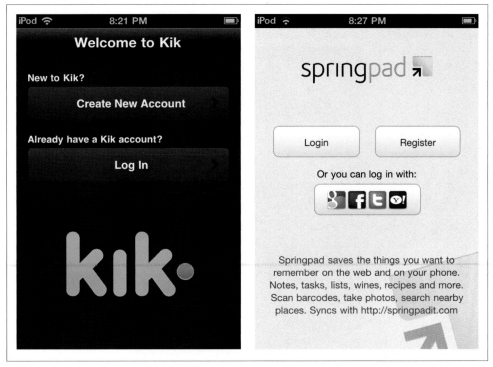

Figure 2-4. kik and springpad

Another pattern is to forgo the user name field and just require a password. The user can be authenticated when the application is installed, and then only prompted for a password to access sensitive data. This is a popular option among financial apps, like PNCs Virtual Wallet, but could be used across industries. Offering a mobile PIN as a password fulfills the same purpose.

Figure 2-5. PNC's VirualWallet

 Don't innovate on the sign in screen, use common practices to make it easy for users to get signed in. Provide a way to retrieve a forgotten password.

Registration

Registration, like Sign In, should have a minimal amount of inputs. Chui Chui Tan recommends ruthlessly editing "elements which do not carry important functions." This might mean eliminating the redundant *confirm email* and *confirm password* fields.

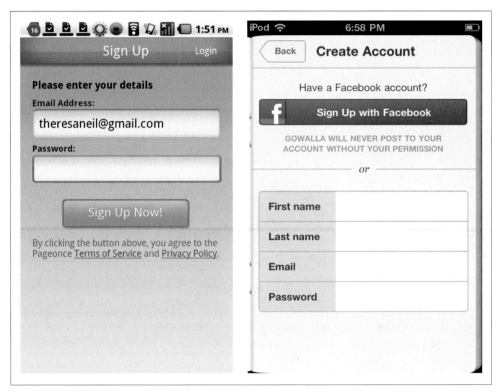

Figure 2-6. PageOnce and Gowalla

Since this may be the first form you design for your application, establish a labeling convention that is easy to read. Avoid horizontal labels and instead use vertical labels, like Evernote, or watermarked field labels, like Intuit.

Figure 2-7. Horizontal labels can end up truncated

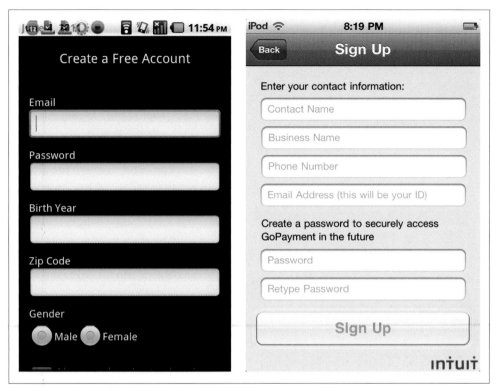

Figure 2-8. Vertical labels and watermark label

Offer inline feedback, when appropriate, like kik does for *User Name* availability. See Chapter 8, for more tips.

Figure 2-9. Inline feedback for user name availability in kik

 Keep it short, preferably one screen, with the Register button above the fold. Make it simple for an already registered use to sign in.

Checkout

At this point in time, mobile checkout is more common in mobile optimized websites than in applications, but the same rules apply to both:

- Use device standard controls in the checkout form.
- Consider consolidating multiple screens into one checkout form. Retailers like Zappos and Apple present a short checkout form with sections that can be drilled into to complete. Other retailers like Target and Gilt simply use a long form.
- Offer a mechanism for a faster checkout in the future, like saved card information, or sign in to checkout.
- Display the security lock in the header to indicate a secure connection.

Checkout wizards, like Home Depot, may not be the fastest, most efficient design. See the Multi-Step pattern for better design options.

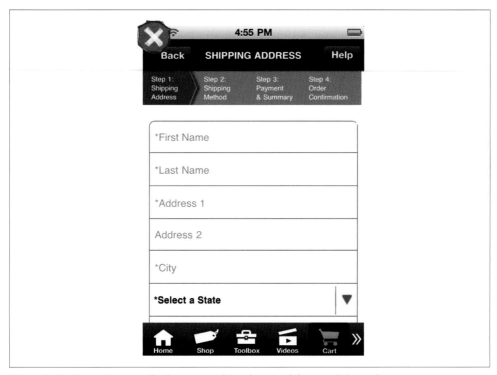

Figure 2-10. Home Depot's checkout wizard is suboptimal for a mobile application

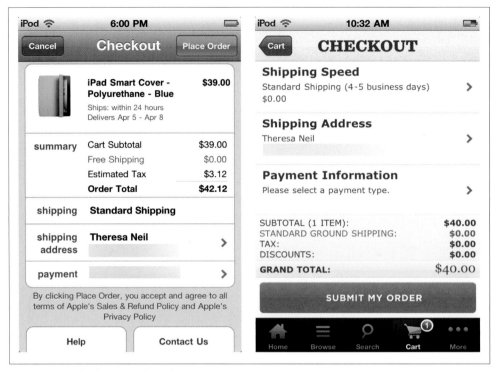

Figure 2-11. Checkout: Apple and Zappos

 Design for speed, efficiency, and reassurance. Eliminate unnecessary fields and minimize the number of pages and steps.

Calculate

Calculator style apps like weight trackers, tax estimators, and loan calculators all require input. And although these forms can use custom controls and layouts, it is still important to follow basic conventions concerning readability.

Figure 2-12. Custom controls: CardioTrainer and WeightBot

Alignment, labels, fonts, button placement, contrast, and colors all affect the usability of mobile forms. For example, compare the readability of the Valspar Paint Calculator, well aligned fields and labels, with that of the Behr Paint Calculator.

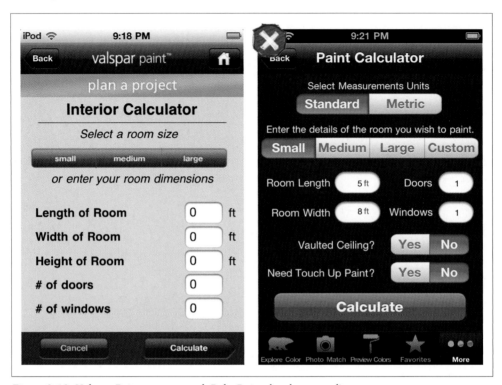

Figure 2-13. Valspar Paint, easy to read; Behr Paint, harder to read'

The best calculation apps tightly correlate the input with a visual result. TaxCaster uses a gauge to visualize taxes due or refund amount, and HypoCalc integrates a chart in the form.

Figure 2-14. TaxCaster and HypoCalc

 Use standard form conventions for design and layout. If possible, visualize the results in the same page.

Search Form

Some searches require multiple inputs, or criteria, to generate results. Like the other form patterns, search criteria should be limited to only the essential fields and provide sensible defaults. For example, Kayak's flight search form defaults to a round-trip ticket, for one person, economy class. They use a custom form layout to keep all the criteria and *search* button above the fold. OpenTable defaults to your current location, date, and upcoming time to search for restaurants you can get a reservation at.

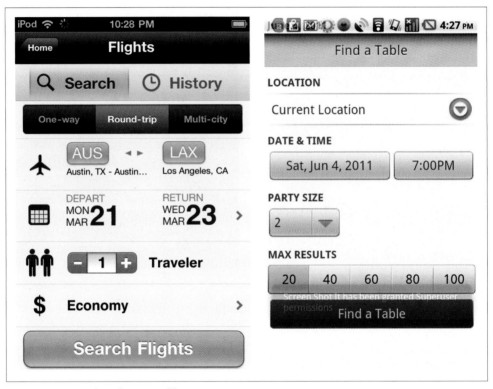

Figure 2-15. Kayak and Open Table

Edmunds' Car Research and New Car Inventory search are also single pages, and they implement a live preview displaying the number of matches before the full search is run.

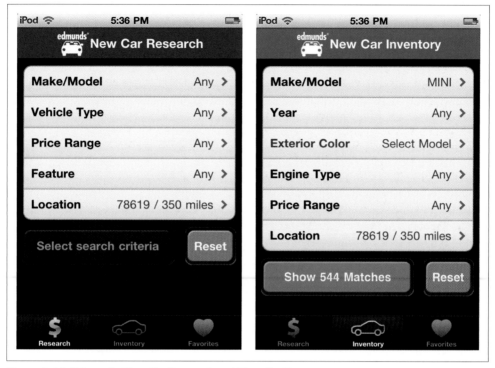

Figure 2-16. Edmund's New Car Research and New Car Inventory

Trulia and REALTOR.com offer similar search criteria, but Trulia's interface is easier to manipulate and less overwhelming than the dozen or so fields in REALTOR.com.

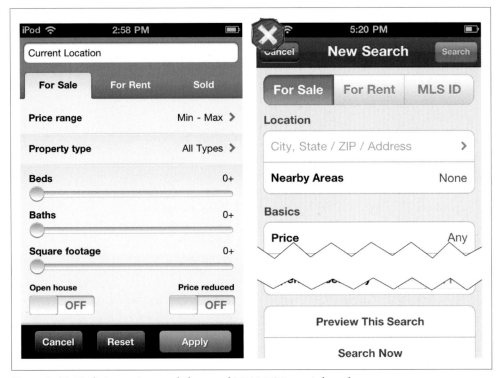

Figure 2-17. Trulia's concise search form and REALTOR.com's long form

 Avoid overwhelming the user with options, aim for a single page of criteria. Use appropriate controls that are finger friendly and fast.

Multi-Step

With smaller screens, mobile devices just don't have the real estate to display the bulky wizards normally associated with multi-step forms on the Web. A simple solution is to show the current step and number of total steps like Fring's registration flow.

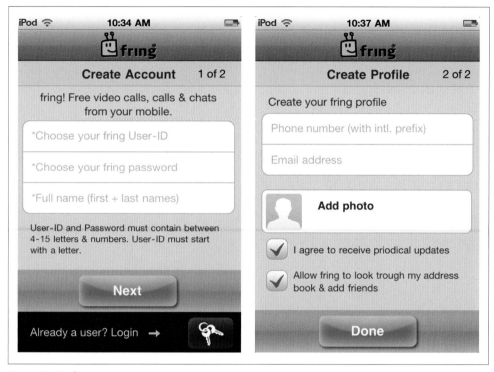

Figure 2-18. fring

More context may be necessary for lengthier flows. Product configurators like Chipotle's online ordering and Starbucks' drink builder guide the user with a *next* or *continue* button. But this approach skirts the fundamental usability rule of navigation: let the user know where they are and where they can go (i.e., step number x of y). Clear navigation is especially important in mobile forms, since there is a higher likelihood of the user being interrupted or otherwise distracted.

Figure 2-19. Chipotle and Starbucks

A better design is the TurboTax SnapTax app, where the steps and submit button are presented on a single page. Each step can be drilled into and completed. This single-page approach provides valuable navigation information (there are three steps in the process, two are remaining), but it also doubles as a concise summary to review before submitting.

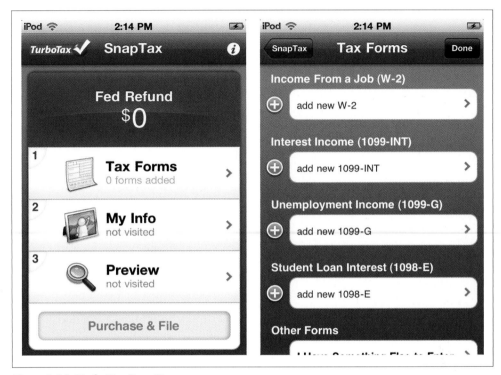

Figure 2-20. TurboTax Snap Tax

Square uses a stylized progress indicator in the title section of the app, providing both a visual indicator of the number of steps, and current step.

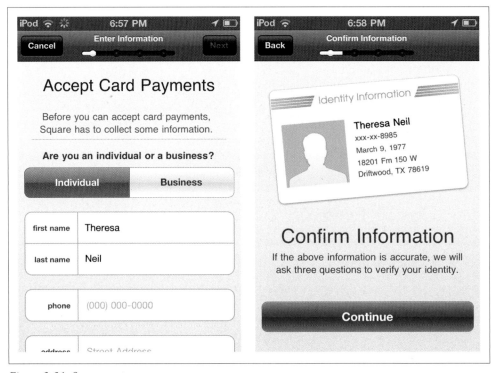

Figure 2-21. Square: set-up process

 Show the user where they are and where they can go. Eliminate unnecessary fields and minimize the number of pages and steps.

Long Form

Some forms will require scrolling. The trickiest part of the Long Form is determining where to put the command and escape buttons. Zappos and Skype both use modal forms in their iOS apps, so the buttons are in the title bar.

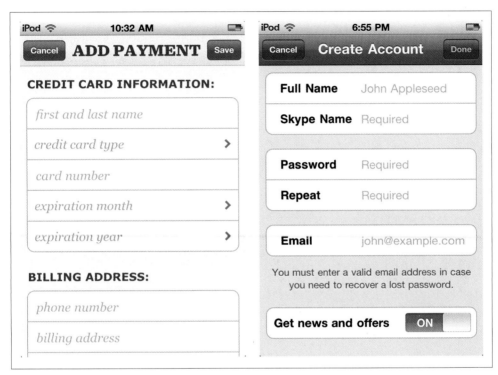

Figure 2-22. Long forms: Zappos and Skype

This would be nonstandard in other OSs, but simply placing the buttons at the bottom of the form works well.

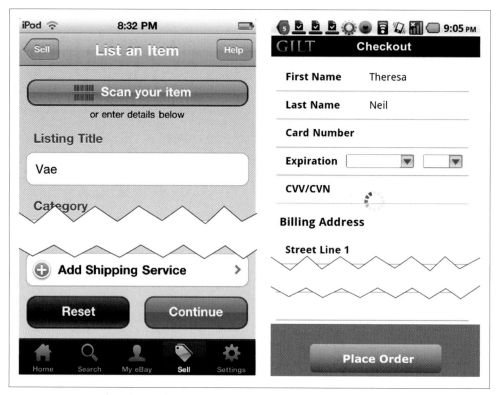

Figure 2-23. eBay's long listing form and Gilt's long checkout form

Follow form design best practices, as well as the guidelines specific to the OS for button order and alignment. Discover Card visually differentiates the command button from the escape button but has them in the wrong order for iOS. Sam's Club has the buttons in the right order, but the buttons have the same visual weight, so you have to look closely to choose the right one.

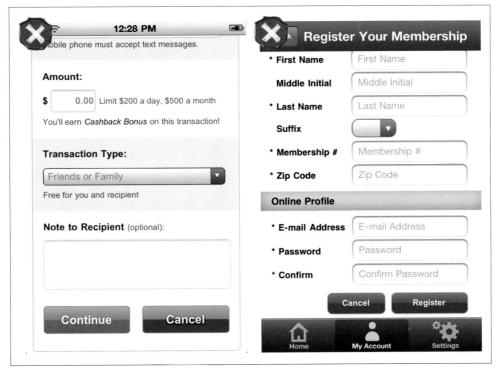

Figure 2-24. Discover, good design, wrong order; Sam's Club, correct layout, bad design

 Don't artificially break the form into steps just to prevent scrolling. Do ruthlessly edit the form for any unnecessary fields. Follow OS standards for button placement.

CHAPTER 3
Tables & Lists

Patterns: Basic Table, Headerless Tables, Grouped Rows, Fixed Column, Cascading Lists, Editable Tables, Tables with Visual Indicators. Overview plus Data

Many of our clients have enterprise applications or robust productivity tools that usually include tables packed full of data. Envision a table with dozens of columns that scrolls horizontally and vertically. They want to know how we're going to get those tables in their mobile app. Well, we're not. At least not in the same way we do on the Web. But the good news is that the mobile form factor gives us an opportunity to reevaluate which information is most important to display.

For example, a long table of student test results might be better represented as a chart that you could drill into to see all students who scored in a certain band of the bell curve:

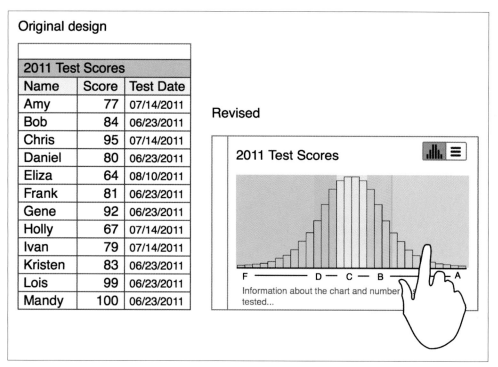

Figure 3-1. Redesigned table

And we can provide an alternate view of the information using a Headerless Table with Dynamic Search for quickly accessing a specific student's results:

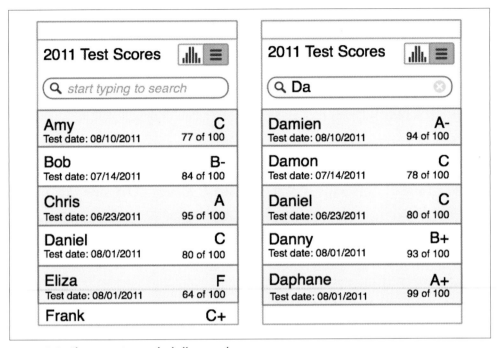

Figure 3-2. Alternate view to the bell curve chart

Once you've identified the key data your app needs to display, check out these table patterns for inspiration:

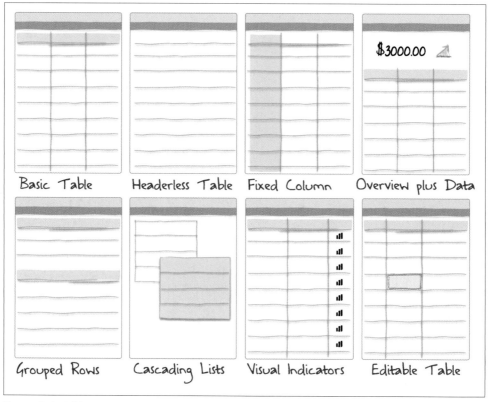

Figure 3-3. Table patterns

Basic Table

This is just a standard table with fixed column headers and a grid layout. Alternating table row colors, also called zebra stripping, or subtle lines between rows may improve the readability of the table.

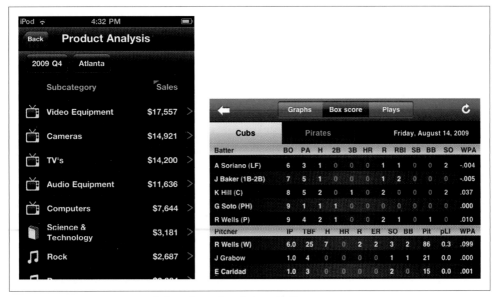

Figure 3-4. MicroStrategy Mobile and FanGraphs Baseball

 Avoid using dark gridlines and vertical dividers. Left align text and right align numbers. Don't overload the screen. Consider an alternate pattern if there is too much information to fit on a single screen.

Headerless Table

The headerless table is characterized by fat rows displaying multiple variables about an object, and no column labels. It is common practice to make the row identifier a larger font and display the details in a smaller font. Realtor.com tests the limits of what you can fit in these fat rows. They probably should have omitted the redundant dwelling type (Single Family, shown truncated as Single... and Single Fam...) description, since that information is clearly communicated in the title above the table.

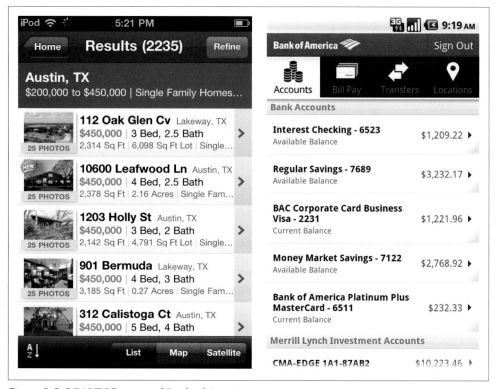

Figure 3-5. REALTOR.com and Bank of America

The pattern is ideal for displaying collections of items (like inventory, recipes, albums, etc.) and search results. Like a list, this pattern is meant for quick scanning and selection.

 Three rows of information maximum per fat row. Use smaller and/or lighter font for less important details. Don't guess what the most important information is, ask your customers and validate the designs.

Fixed Column

For larger tables, the fixed column pattern may be a viable solution. In this example from Roambi, the leftmost column is frozen and the rest of the columns scroll. Fidelity uses fixed columns on the left and right with scrolling content in the center, but this design is harder to navigate than Roambi's, since there is a smaller target for swiping.

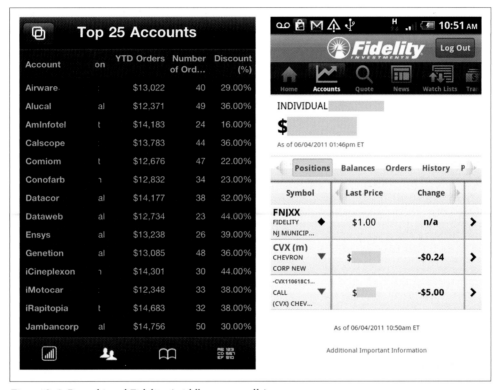

Figure 3-6. Roambi and Fidelity (middle area scrolls)

Provide visual affordance which column is fixed, and that swiping can reveal more data.

Overview plus Data

The Overview plus Data pattern refers to a roll-up or summary of the table's content displayed above the individual rows of data. My favorite example of this in a web app is in Discover's SpendAnalyzer.

Figure 3-7. Discover SpendAnalyzer

In mobile apps, like Bank of America's accounts page, the available balance in the savings account (overview) is shown in large font over the account details (data). In the other example from NASDAQ.com, the overview is fixed above the content, so you can scroll through the portfolio without loosing the summary.

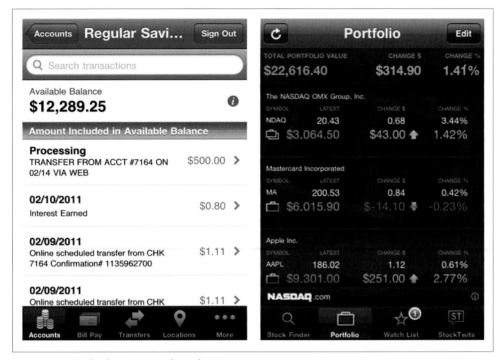

Figure 3-8. Bank of America and QFolio

Adobe Site Catalyst uses a graph for the summary; however, the pie chart design needs improvement since the legend is illegible. Proofpoint does a nice job of incorporating the legend with the data.

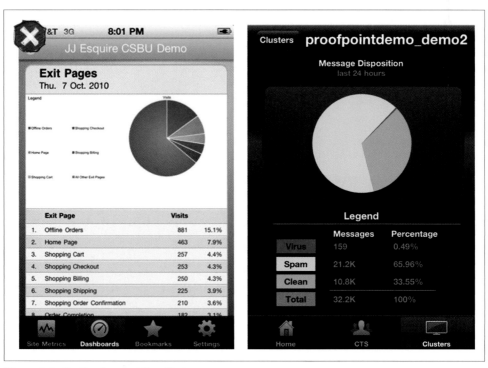

Figure 3-9. SiteCatalyst and ProofPoint

 The overview should be presented above the data and be easy to understand at a glance.

Grouped Rows

Row grouping can make a table's data easier to digest. The row groupings might act as section headers, like transactions grouped by date in the Mint example, or as subsection summaries, like the yellow total rows in the MicroStrategy Mobile example.

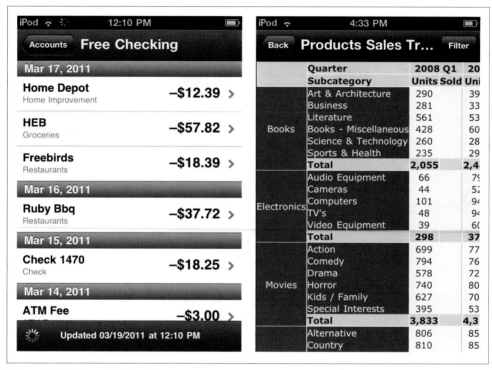

Figure 3-10. Mint and MicroStrategy

 Visually differentiate the summary rows from the other rows in the table.

Cascading Lists

For obvious reasons, a tree table would be pretty cumbersome on a phone screen, but a cascading list can provide the same hierarchal structure. This cascading list in Wine Spectator makes it easy to navigate from country to variety to the vintage table.

Figure 3-11. WineSpectator

iOS refers to this as a Table View, a UI element that "presents data in a single-column list of multiple rows." DropBox uses this pattern for their secondary navigation within the DropBox tab.

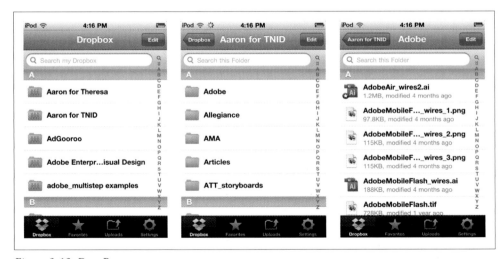

Figure 3-12. DropBox

Use a fairly flat information hierarchy to avoid deep drilling (more than three levels) in the application. Deep drilling may not be avoidable if the Cascading List pattern is used to navigate a user defined information hierarchy.

Table with Visual Indicators

Sparklines and icons can enhance a table's information display, making it easier to hone in on specific items of interest. My Diet Calendar uses color-coded arrows to show if my net caloric intake is higher or lower than what I have expended for the day. The Roambi Sales by Store table uses sparklines plus icons to show the shape of the monthly sales numbers and trends.

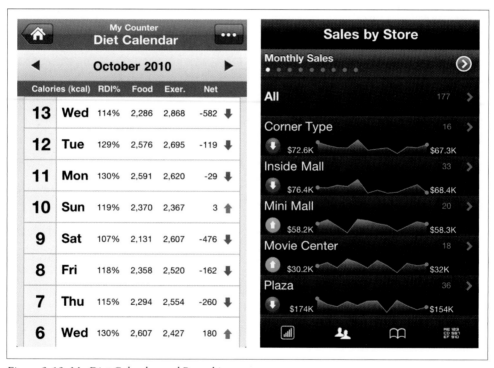

Figure 3-13. My Diet Calendar and Roambi

See Chapter 6, for more information about sparklines in mobile apps.

 Choose visual indicators that are immediately recognizable; avoid gratuitous icon use.

Editable Table

Editable tables in mobile interfaces are almost exclusively found in spreadsheet applications like QuickOffice. Many of the same guidelines for editable tables on the Web apply to mobile:

- Clearly indicate the cell and/or row selected.
- If there is a specific format for the cell, offer the appropriate editor (selector, spinner, color picker, date picker...).
- Provide feedback and error messages onSave, not onChange.

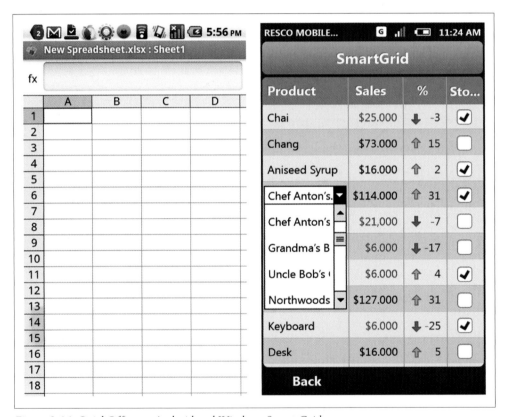

Figure 3-14. QuickOffice on Android and Windows Smart Grid

Unlike on the Web, editable tables on mobile devices are not appropriate for extensive data entry since keyboard navigation (specifically tabbing) isn't supported by most mobile keyboards.

Leverage web and desktop design best practices for editable tables. Avoid using editable tables for bulk data entry, or when extensive amounts of edits could be necessary.

CHAPTER 4

Search, Sort & Filter

Patterns: Explicit Search, Auto-complete, Scoped Search, Saved & Recent, Search Criteria (form), Search Results, Onscreen Sort, Sort Order Selector, Sort Form, Onscreen filter, Filter Drawer, Filter Dialog, Filter Form

As I was waiting for a table at a local restaurant the other day, I flipped through a couple of the free classified papers. I was shocked to realize how dependent I've grown on three simple features that just aren't available in a paper-based model: search, sort, and filter.

AutoDirect and some of the other freebies may be organized by category (like trucks, vans, SUVs) but others like Greensheet just list page after page of items for sale. I would actually have to read every single ad in the paper to see if anyone was selling what I wanted. No thank you. I'll use Craig's List on my phone instead.

But this got me thinking. While we take search, sort, and filter for granted in our digital world, there are some nuances to getting it right in a mobile application. This chapter explores a dozen plus different approaches to search, sort, and filter in mobile applications.

Search

Peter Morville and Jeffery Callendar provide an excellent summary of design patterns for searching in *Search Patterns: Design for Discovery* (O'Reilly), January 2010 (*http://shop.oreilly.com/product/9780596802288.do*). I highly recommend reading this book before designing any search interface, whether for mobile or other platforms.

In this section, we'll look at search patterns specific to mobile applications including patterns for:

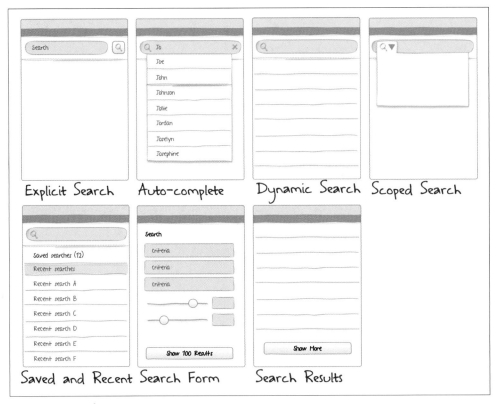

Figure 4-1. Search patterns

Explicit Search

Explicit search relies on an explicit action to perform the search and view results. That action might be to tap a search button on the screen, like Walmart, or on the keyboard, like Target. The results are typically displayed in the area below the search bar. Consider pairing an explicit search pattern with the auto-complete pattern.

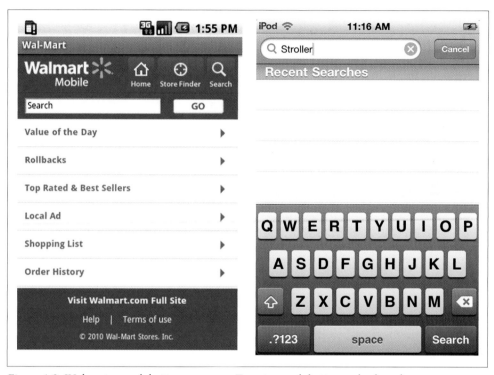

Figure 4-2. Walmart, search button on screen; Target, search button on keyboard

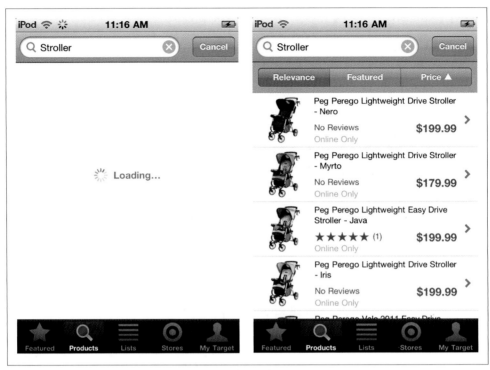

Figure 4-3. Target, loading and displaying search results

  Offer a clear button in the field and an option to cancel the search. Use feedback to show the search is being performed (see Chapter 8).

Search with Auto-Complete

Probably the most widely adopted search pattern in web and mobile apps is auto-complete. Typing will immediately surface a set of possible results, just tap on one to selected it, and the search will be performed. Or continue typing and tap the explicit search button.

Figure 4-4. Android Marketplace and Netflix

Ideally, the results will be displayed immediately, but a progress indicator (searching...) should be used for system feedback. Netflix (above) uses an indicator in the search field, whereas Fidelity (below) displays one where the results will eventually be displayed.

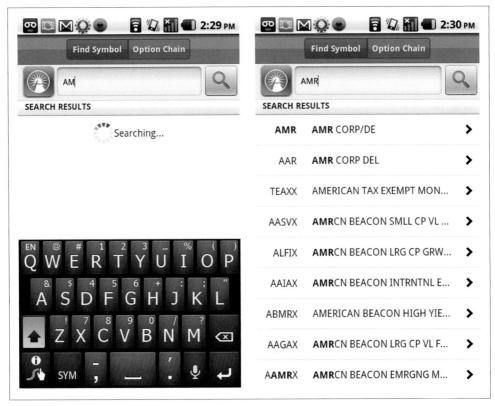

Figure 4-5. Fidelity

TripAdvisor provides an enhanced auto-complete, grouping the results by popular destinations, hotels, restaurants...

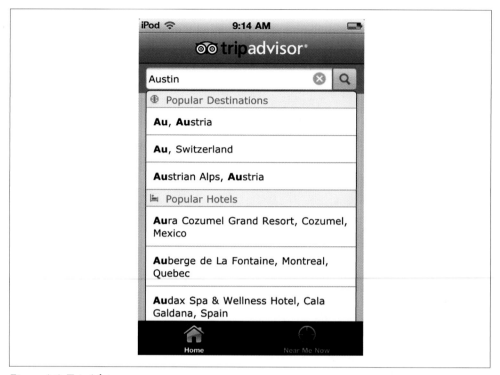

Figure 4-6. TripAdvisor

 Show feedback if there could be a delay in displaying the results. Consider emphasizing the matching search text in the search results.

Dynamic Search

This pattern may also be considered dynamic filtering. Entering search text will dynamically filter the data on the screen. In these examples from BlackBerry App World and People on webOS, entering text filters the existing list of items.

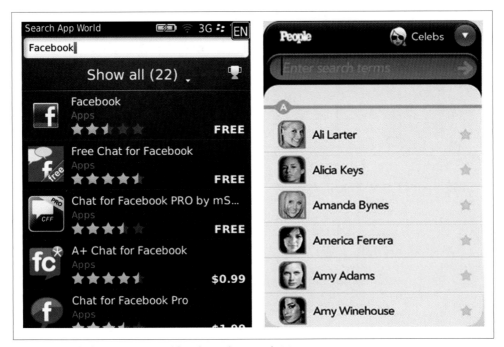

Figure 4-7. BlackBerry App World and People on WebOS

 Works well for constrained data sets, like an address book or personal media library, but may be impractical for searching huge data sets.

Scoped Search

Sometimes it is easier (and faster) to get to the desired result by scoping the search criteria before performing the search. Google and Photobucket use different designs to the same end.

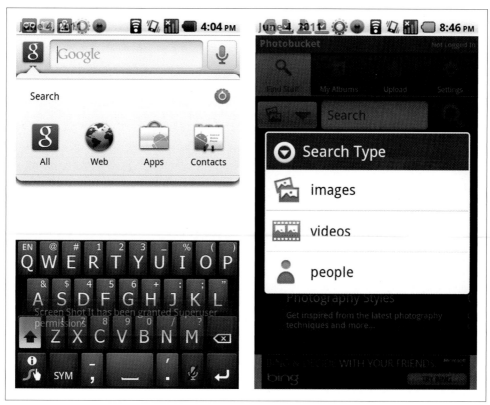

Figure 4-8. Google and Photobucket

AllRecipes also lets you select criteria (or filters) before submitting the search. Dropbox defaults the initial scope to *All*, but you can switch it to *Files* or *Folders* before or after tapping the *search* button.

Figure 4-9. AllRecipes and DropBox

 Offer reasonable scoping options based on the data set. Three to six scoping options are plenty; consider a search form for advanced searching capabilities.

Saved and Recent Searches

Successful mobile interfaces follow a basic usability maxim: respect the users' effort. Saved and recent searches do this by making it easy to select from previous searches, instead of retyping the same keywords or search criteria. eBay and Walmart both use Saved and Recent Searches to increase users' efficiency.

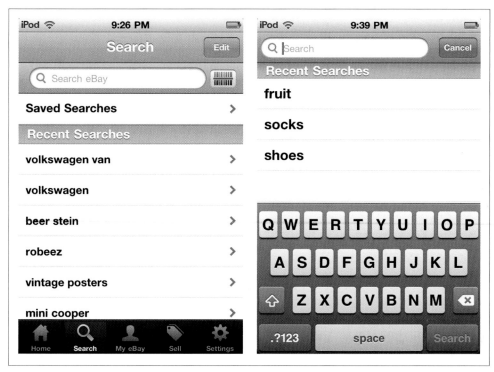

Figure 4-10. eBay and Walmart

Other options to respect the users' effort involve location-based searching options like Trulia, and bar code searching, like PriceCheck by Amazon.

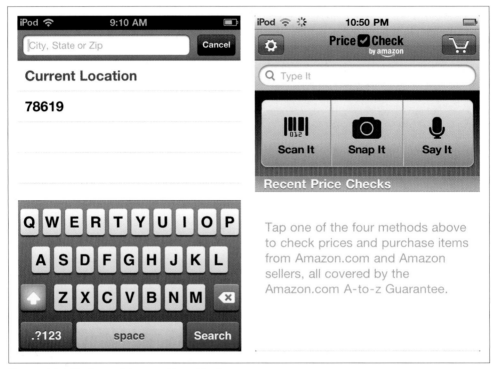

Figure 4-11. Trulia and Amazon PriceCheck

 Saved searches typically require additional steps for naming a search for reference later, whereas recent searches are implicitly saved and surfaced. Consider which one will best serve your users' needs.

Search Form

This pattern is characterized by a separate form for entering multiple criteria, and an explicit search button. Kayak and Whole Foods use search forms to collect the necessary criteria for searching for flights and hotels. See more examples in Chapter 2.

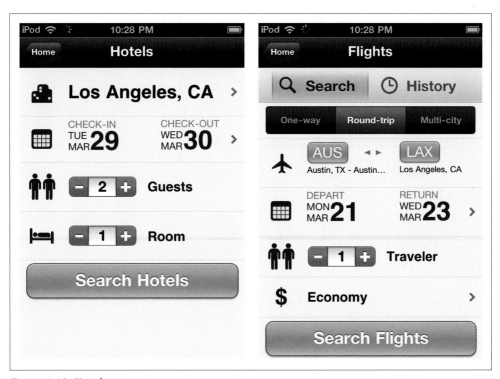

Figure 4-12. Kayak

Figure 4-13. Whole Foods Recipe Search

 Minimize the number of input fields. Implement OS-specific input controls properly. Follow form design best practices (alignment, labels, size).

Search Results/View Results

Once a search is performed, the results can be displayed in the same screen or on a dedicated results screen. Results may be displayed in a table or list, on a map or satellite, or as thumbnail images. Multiple view options can be used, depending on the type of results and user preferences.

Figure 4-14. Results in a table: Kayak and Foursquare

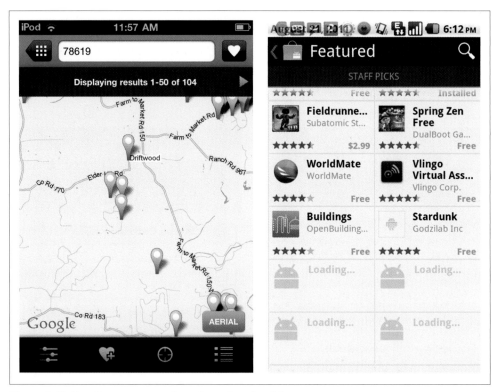

Figure 4-15. Results on a map and results as thumbnail images

Lazy loading is a common technique to use so that some results will be displayed while the rest are being loaded, see Ebay Motors and BestBuy. Many applications offer either a button to explicitly "view more results" or will automatically load more results when the screen is flicked.

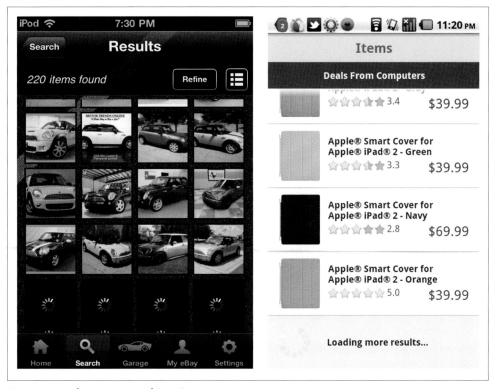

Figure 4-16. ebay Motors and Best Buy

Avoid paging tables, they break the natural interaction model of viewing information on a mobile device.

 Label the results with the number returned. Use lazy loading instead of paging. Apply a reasonable default sort order.

Sort Patterns

It is important to choose a reasonable default sort for displaying search results. A little common sense plus user validation is the best way to choose the default sort order. To offer additional sorting functionality, choose an existing interface design pattern:

- onscreen sort
- sort order selector
- the sort form

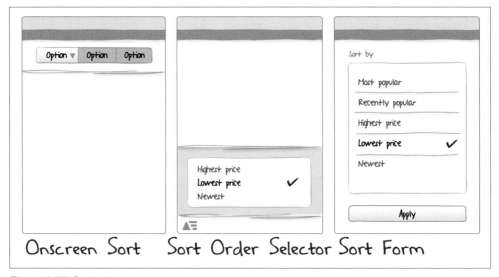

Figure 4-17. Sort patterns

Onscreen Sort

When there are only a few sort options, an onscreen sort can provide a simple one-tap solution. Placing the sort toggle at the top or bottom of the screen will depend on the other screen elements.

Target provides four sort options with a three-toggle button. For the price sort option, they offer two choices: sort by price ascending and sort by price descending.

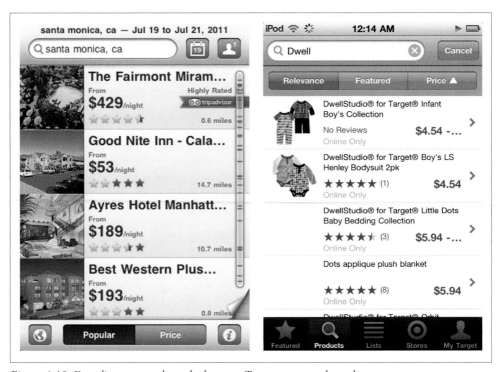

Figure 4-18. Expedia, sort toggle at the bottom; Target, sort toggle at the top

 Clearly show which option is selected or "on." Consider the Sort Order Selector pattern if the option labels don't fit nicely in a toggle button bar.

Sort Order Selector

The selector pattern is a good alternative to the onscreen sort. There are a number of different UI controls that can be used for selection, but consider the design guidelines for the OS you are designing for (for example, the menu is common for Android app, and the picker and actionsheet are common in iOS apps).

The option titles can be longer (more explicit), and more options can be displayed. Walmart places the sort button in proximity with the search field, whereas Realtor.com puts it down with the other view options and actions

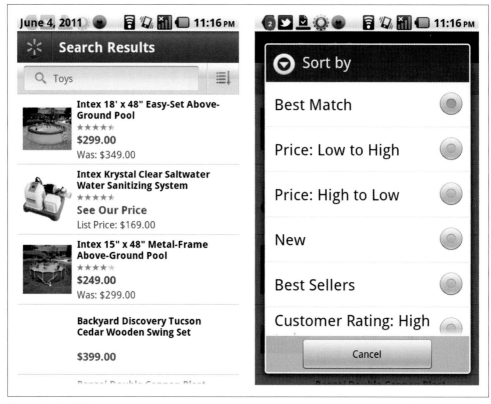

Figure 4-19. Walmart

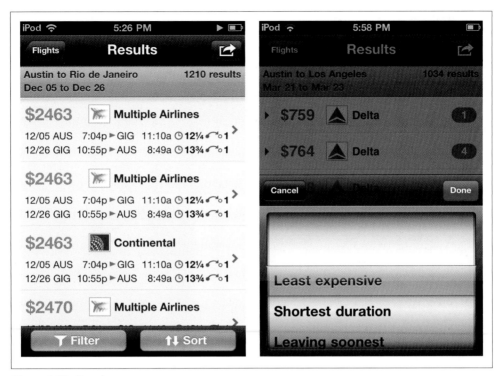

Figure 4-20. Kayak

OS neutral solutions include a simple combobox, like Target, or an overlay menu, like Awesome Note.

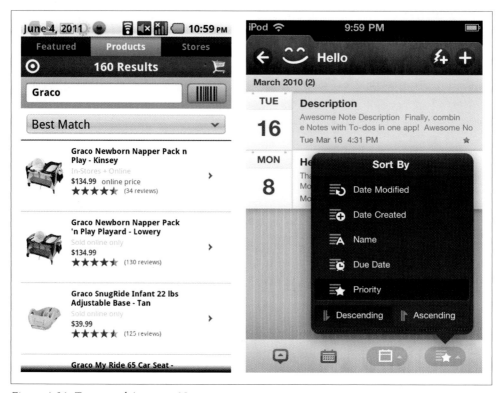

Figure 4-21. Target and Awesome Note

 Follow OS design conventions for choosing the selector control, or choose an OS neutral interface control. Clearly show which sort option is applied.

Sort Form

Some applications have consolidated the sort and filter options into one screen, typically titled "Refine." This is the most effort intensive sort pattern, requiring the user to open the form, select an option, and then apply the selection (by tapping "done" or "apply").

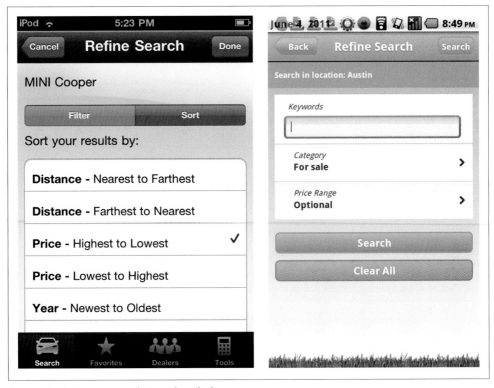

Figure 4-22. Cars.com and eBay classifieds

 Consider the more efficient sort option toggle or sort order selector patterns before choosing this pattern.

Filter

Large sets of data can require additional filtering, also called *refining*. Filtering relies on the user selecting criteria by which to refine the set of search results or a large set of objects. Common filtering patterns include:

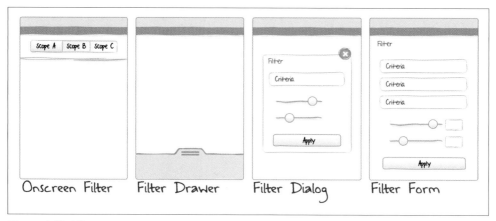

Figure 4-23. Filter patterns

Also see the earlier search pattern, Scoped Search, for an optional pre-filtering technique.

Onscreen Filter

Similar to the onscreen sort, the onscreen filter is displayed with the results or list of objects. With one tap, the filter is applied. HeyZap uses the standard toggle button bar, whereas Google uses vertical tabs.

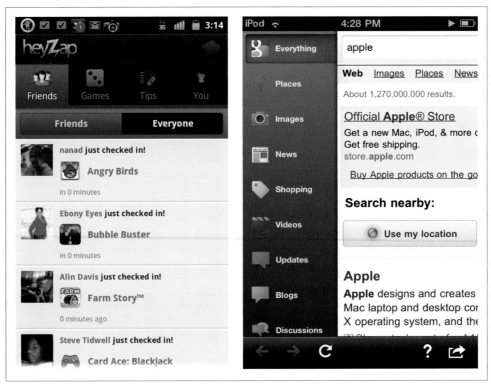

Figure 4-24. HeyZap and Google

CBS News and the ACL Festival app use a scrolling filter bar as a way to let users quickly hone in on certain types of articles and bands, respectively.

Don't use this filter pattern for primary navigation, but instead use it to group and filter content. See Chapter 10, Metaphor Mismatch.

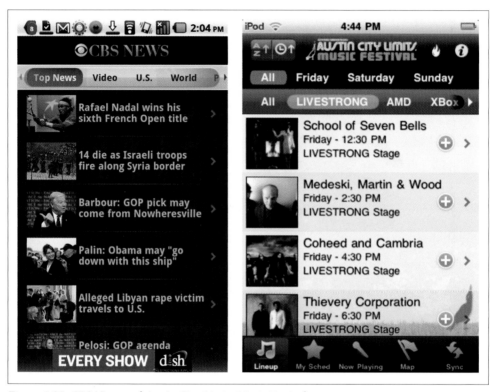

Figure 4-25. CBS News and Austin City Limits Music Festival

SXSW offers a filter button bar combined with a second row of filtering options. Feed a Fever news reader uses a super simple stylized set of comboboxes for filtering news feeds.

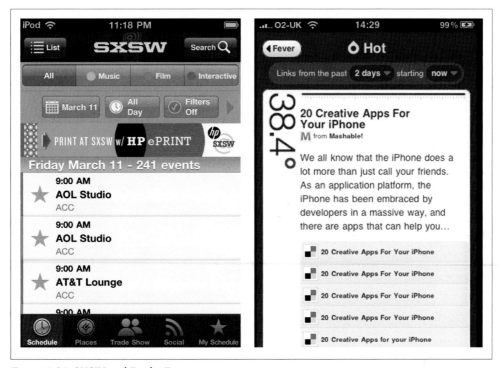

Figure 4-26. SXSW and Feed a Fever

 Filter options should be clearly worded and easy to understand. Show the filters that are applied, or "on."

Filter Drawer

Almost as efficient as the onscreen filter, a drawer can be used to reveal filter options. Flicking or tapping a handle will open the drawer. Audible's drawer reveals a simple filter toggle bar, whereas Sam's offers a host of filter options that can be applied to the map of club locations. A better design for Sam's would be to leave the map visible and allow for dynamic filtering instead of the explicit "filter" button.

Figure 4-27. Audible and Sam's Club

Filter Dialog

Like a pop-up on in a web app, the filter dialog is modal in nature. It requires the user to select a filter option, or cancel the action. TripAdvisor on iOS has a custom filter dialog, whereas USPS Mobile on Android relies on the default selector control.

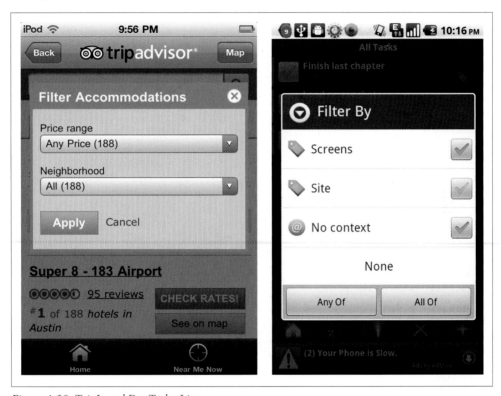

Figure 4-28. TripIt and DueTodayLite

While the Filter Dialog may get the job done, the first two patterns provide more freedom for users to experiment with and apply filters directly in context.

 Keep the options list short, avoid scrolling. Consider a Filter Form for lengthier or multi-select filter options. See Chapter 6, Charts with Filters, for examples on filtering chart data.

Filter Form

Large data sets can benefit from more advanced filter/refinement options. For example, Kayak uses a form to filter hotels based on price, brand, and stars. Zappos uses a similar approach, using the iOS standard clear/done buttons in the title bar.

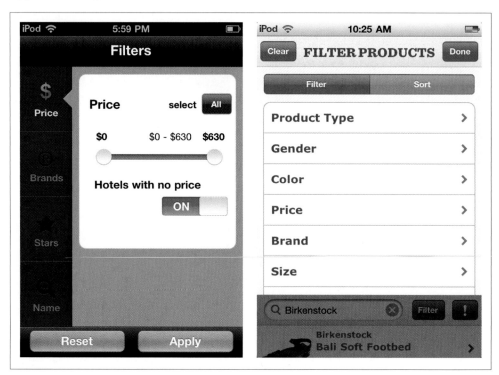

Figure 4-29. Kayak and Zappos

Freetime uses custom controls in their filter form. First you pick the filter category, then choose the filter criteria, then apply the filter to the calendar.

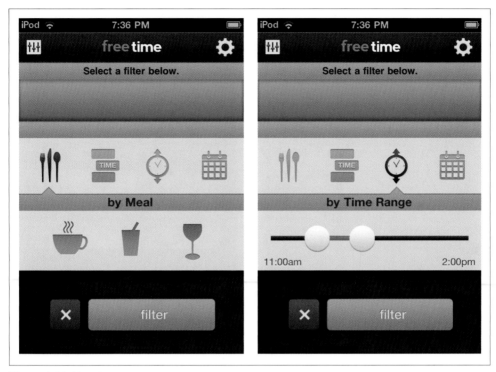

Figure 4-30. Freetime

Conditional filters, also called *predicate editors* or *expression builders*, are an advanced filtering feature typically found in reporting tools. Here's the standard layout used on the Web and desktop.

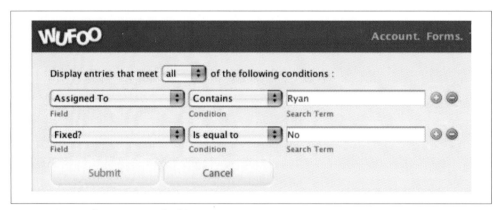

Figure 4-31. Wufoo expression builder

Creating a conditional filtering a mobile application can be challenging because of the form factor, but Roambi has successfully accomplished it.

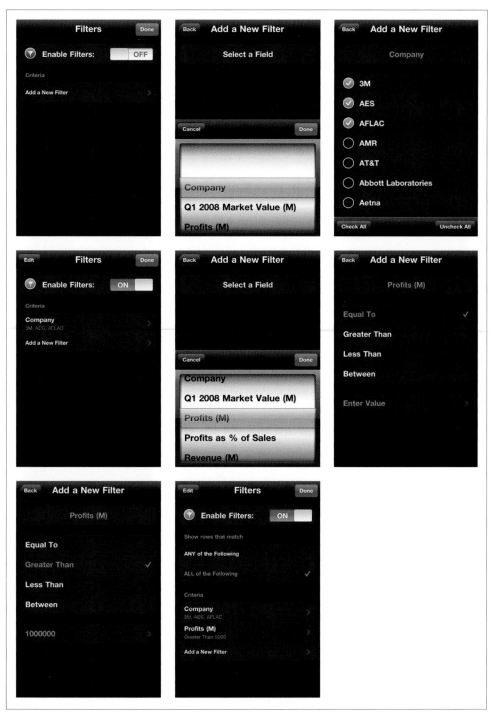

Figure 4-32. Roambi's conditional filter

Don't over-design the filters; a simple onscreen filter or drawer will usually suffice. If a Filter Form is necessary, follow form design best practices.

CHAPTER 5

Tools

Patterns: Toolbar, Overlay Menu, Contextual Tools, Inline Actions, Call to Action Button, Bulk Actions

In *Designing Web Interfaces*(*http://shop.oreilly.com/product/9780596516253.do*) (O'Reilly), Bill Scott and I wrote of six principles for designing rich interactions on the Web. Two of these core principles, Make It Direct and Keep It Lightweight, can also help drive the design of tools and actions in mobile interfaces.

Make It Direct suggests providing input where there is output; the interface should respond directly to the users' interaction. A good example on the Web is Flickr's inline editing.

Figure 5-1. Inline edit on Flickr

Keep It Lightweight refers to keeping the interaction as lightweight as possible. An early example of this principle in action on the Web was Digg. The one-step process to Digg an article had a huge impact on the success of the site.

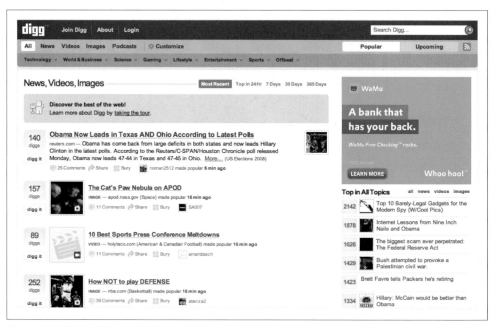

Figure 5-2. Digg's lightweight "Digg It" button

I've been thinking about both principles quite a bit as I follow Josh Clark's *Buttons are a Hack* campaign. He writes:

> **"Buttons are a hack.** As in the real world, they're often necessary, but they work at a distance—secondary tools to work on primary objects. A light switch here turns on a lightbulb there. These indirect interactions must be learned; they're not contextually obvious. The revolution that touchscreen devices are working is that they allow us, more and more, to use primary content as a control, to create the illusion of direct interaction.
>
> I don't mean to suggest that we throw out all of our familiar buttons entirely. Light switches shall remain necessary, after all, and so shall buttons, especially where it's necessary to trigger abstract actions ("share via Twitter," for example). But it's important to recognize those devices for what they are: necessary hacks for moments when direct interaction isn't possible. Touchscreen interfaces allow that direct interaction in many more contexts. As new solutions arise, we should be open to putting our time-tested workarounds aside. When designing an interaction for touch, always ask: do I really need another button or control for this?"

Take for example Photoshop Express. This mobile app uses the old desktop and web conventions for cropping, straightening, rotating, and flipping an image.

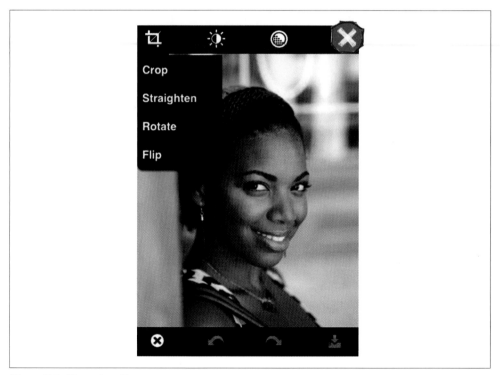

Figure 5-3. Photoshop Express

Tap'n'Scrap instead allows for direct interaction with the image. I can pinch zoom to enlarge, drop on a frame to crop, and drag to rotate or straighten. I can imagine using the flick gesture to flip the image, although they don't have that implemented.

Figure 5-4. Tap'n'Scrap provides direct manipulation of the image

If a button or control is truly necessary in your mobile app, consider these patterns:

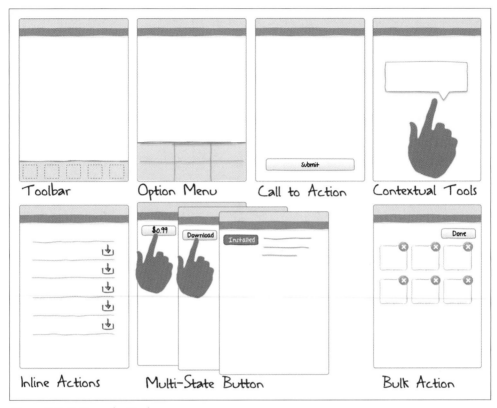

Figure 5-5. Patterns for Tools

Toolbar

The toolbar, also called an action bar, contains tools for screen-level actions. In Pandora, the toolbar includes options for switching to the list view, rating the song, pausing or skipping ahead. A+ Picture Effects for BlackBerry also provides a toolbar of common actions.

Figure 5-6. Pandora and A+Picture Effects

The default style in iOS is the pale blue bar, but it can be stylized.

Figure 5-7. Default iOS toolbar and stylized toolbar in Trip Journal

Sometimes the actions may have additional options to be specified. An OS neutral approach to display a selected tool's options is with a cascading menu. Many mobile applications use this technique to offer editing and formatting options.

Figure 5-8. QuickOffice Pro and Document To Go

Evernote uses a different technique to provide rich text formatting options: an inlay panel that remains visible.

Figure 5-9. Evernote

Actionsheets in iOS are another way to offer more options for a selected tool. Pulse implemented it correctly displaying the four different ways to share a story. Yelp! and Ibis missed the mark by using the actionsheet to show sorting and filtering options, respectively. See Chapter 4, for better ways to sort and filter.

Figure 5-10. Pulse, Ibis, and Yelp

 Toolbars are generally displayed at the bottom of the screen and contain screen-level actions. Choose icons that are familiar and easy to recognize, or use labels plus icons.

Option Menu

Option Menus, like Toolbars, can contain screen-level actions, but can be accessed and displayed in a number of different ways. Android menus are accessed with a hard menu button, but other menus might be opened by flicking a handle or tapping a menu button on the screen.

Figure 5-11. Menu on Android and play menu on Audible

Figure 5-12. Tap Forms and Berry Record

 Choose direct interactions when possible. Don't hide navigation in the Option Menu. Consider the Call to Action Button pattern if you have a single action for the screen.

Call to Action Button

A Call to Action Button may be a better option than a toolbar or a menu when you have only one primary call to action on the screen. Apps including Groupon, Gilt, Expedia, and Foursquare have opted for this pattern instead of a traditional toolbar or option menu.

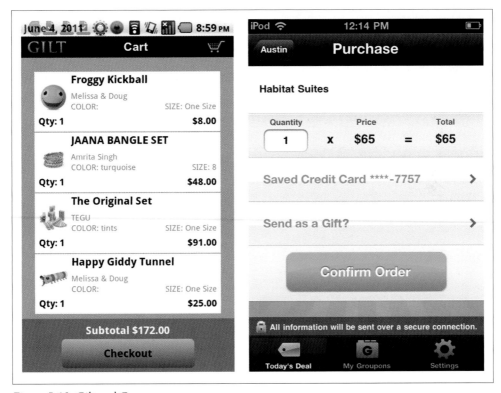

Figure 5-13. Gilt and Groupon

Figure 5-14. Expedia and Foursquare

This pattern may also work for screens with one primary and one ancillary call to action, like Bill Minder. But in these circumstances, visually differentiate the primary call to action from the other button.

Figure 5-15. BillMinder and Netflix

 Don't hide the main call to action in a menu or disguise it as an unrecognizable icon in a toolbar. Make it obvious (good contrast) and spell it out (clear label).

Contextual Tools

Contextual tools can be used to work on a particular object on the screen. It makes sense (and de-clutters the interface) if we only show these tools once the context has been established. For example, a long press on an object (an Android-specific gesture) will reveal charting options in ChartDroid, or tapping on a tweet in Tweed on WebOS will reveal a list of options.

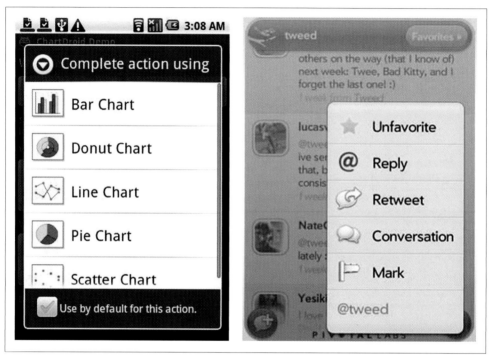

Figure 5-16. ChartDroid and Tweed

Figure 5-17. Mail on Android and iFiles

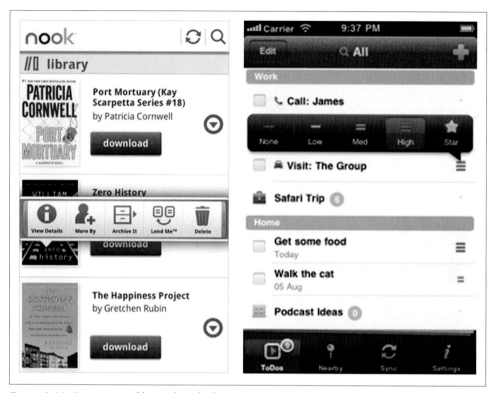

Figure 5-18. Barnes & Noble Nook and 2doApp

Contextual tools can be modal, like the previous examples, or nonmodal, like Daily-Burn and twittermobile.

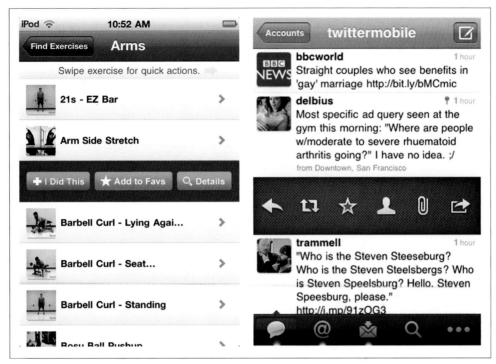

Figure 5-19. DailyBurn and twittermobile

 Choose direct interactions when possible. If buttons are necessary, they should be displayed in proximity to the actionable object. Choose a familiar icon or use a text label.

Inline Actions

Inline actions can also be used to work on a particular object on the screen, but unlike the previous pattern, these actions are always visible. For example, the *download* buttons in Audible and *buy* buttons on Teleflora.

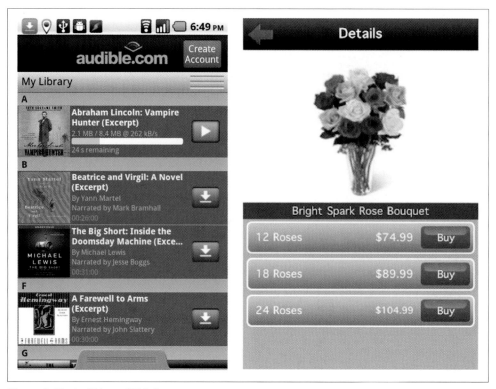

Figure 5-20. Audible and Teleflora

Many applications rely on state-full buttons for the inline actions, like the *add* button in ACL that changes to *remove*, and the *favorites star* button in OpenCaching that can be toggled on or off. See the next pattern, the Multi-State Button, for incorporating more than two states.

Figure 5-21. ACL Music Festival and OpenCaching

 Choose direct interactions when possible. The actions should be in proximity to the actionable object. Choose a familiar icon or use a text label. Max one to two inline actions per object.

Multi-State Button

Normally user interface controls should have a single purpose. However, the Multi-State Button is an exception. In the reduce real-estate of a mobile screen, it may make sense to have the button act as both a trigger and feedback mechanism.

Take for example the experience of downloading a story in Audible. First you'll see the inline action to download a story. Tap it again to download. Then it becomes an indicator for the download progress with an option to swipe and cancel, or play the story.

Figure 5-22. Audible

The Apple App Store and Android Market use this pattern for Buy and Update buttons.

Figure 5-23. Android Market

Another common case for a Multi-State Button is to delete or remove an object. It would break the users' flow to pop up a delete confirmation, see Chapter 10, Idiot Boxes. But it makes sense to require confirmation before an irreparable action is taken.

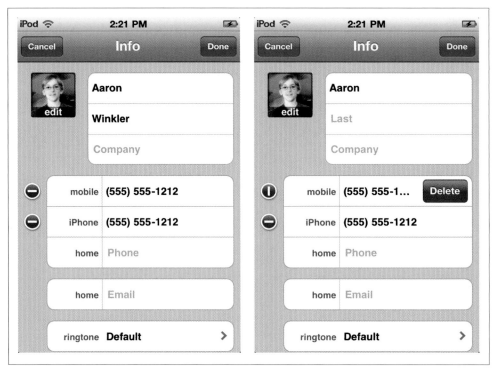

Figure 5-24. Contacts on iOS

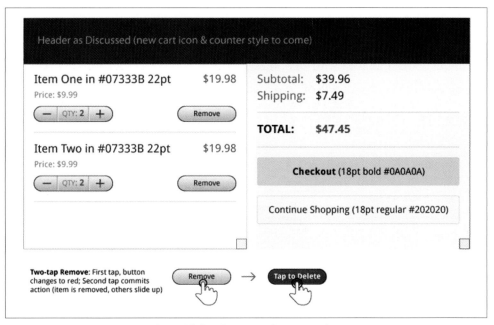

Figure 5-25. Interaction notes from Adobe Flex 4.5 Reference application

Multi-State Buttons work well for a series of tightly correlated actions that will to be performed in succession with limited screen real-estate.

Bulk Actions

Common bulk actions include: selection, adding/deleting, and reordering. Instead of cluttering the main screen with all of these options, provide a mode for bulk actions.

The native Photos app for iOS offers a "selection" mode for choosing photos from the camera roll to share. Likewise, Animoto provides a mode for reordering, and/or removing, clips in a video.

Figure 5-26. Photos on iOS and Animoto

ShoppingList has a simple design for editing a list:

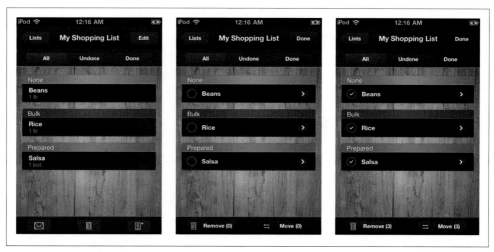

Figure 5-27. Shopping List

And tools like Path and Pulse will provide simple configuration screens for bulk actions like add, remove, and reorder.

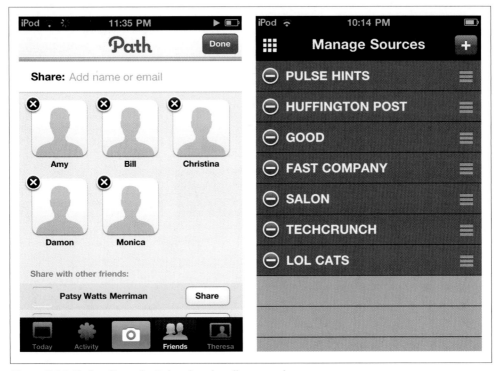

Figure 5-28. Path, edit mode; Pulse, drag handle to reorder sources

 Bulk actions like delete and reorder are best handled in an edit mode. Provide an obvious option for exiting the mode.

CHAPTER 6

Charts

Patterns: Chart with Filters, Overview + Data, Scrolling with Preview, Data Point Details, Drill Down, Zoom In, Pivot Table, Sparklines

Mobile chart design inherits many of the same guidelines and best practices as print and desktop chart design. A great introductory book for this topic is *The Wall Street Journal Guide to Information Graphics: The Dos and Don'ts of Presenting Data, Facts, and Figures*, by Dona M. Wong. I also recommend Stephen Few's books on chart design.

All of these patterns build on a basic chart design. At a minimum, charts should include a title, axis labels, and data. The data may be displayed as a pie, bar, column, area, line, bubble, scatter plot, bullet, radar, gauge, or mixed chart. Depending on the type of chart, a legend may be necessary.

Some basic charts are used in RunKeeper Pro and GasLog to illustrate a runner's pace over the course of their run, and cost of gas over time, respectively.

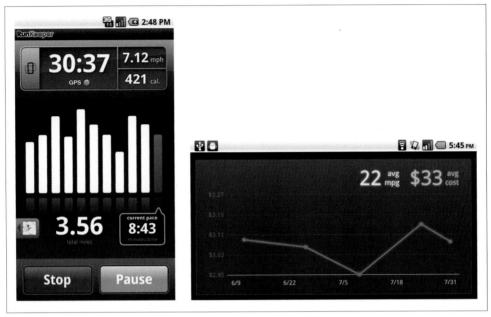

Figure 6-1. RunKeepr Pro and Gas Log

Once the basic chart design is established, watch for *Chart Junk* that might sneak in. Chart Junk refers to visual elements in charts and graphs that are not necessary to comprehend the information represented on the graph or that distract the viewer from this information [wikipedia]. See Chapter 10, for more information on Chart Junk.

Another tip to consider before opening up Photoshop is to get familiar with the charting library your developers will be using. Some libraries like ZingChart and Sencha Touch Charts have good charts right out of the box, others may require custom code to make them usable.

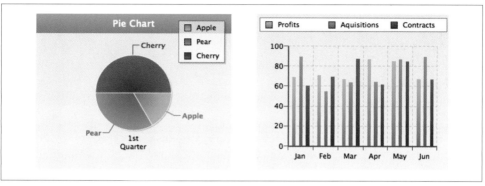

Figure 6-2. ZingCharts

Patterns we'll explore in this chapter include:

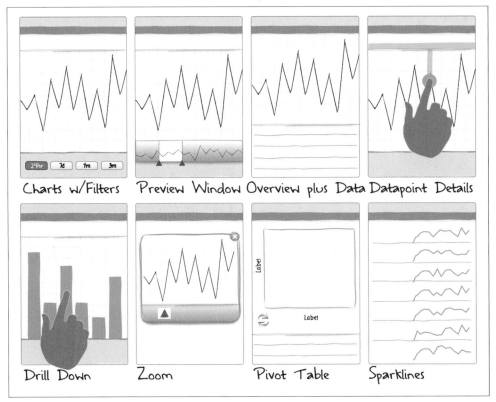

Figure 6-3. Patterns for charts

Chart with Filters

A basic chart can be enhanced with time controls or other filtering capabilities. In these examples from Fidelity and AccuFuel, the data can be analyzed from different time frames.

Figure 6-4. Fidelity and AccuFuel

If you're going to offer time control filters, provide plenty of space for the touch target. In this example from Chaikin, it is difficult to even see the filter controls since they are in the chart.

Figure 6-5. Chaikin

I recommend bottom-aligned controls, like SmartGlance and Blue Mobile, because they are easier to access with the thumb and don't require the user to cover up the data with their hand.

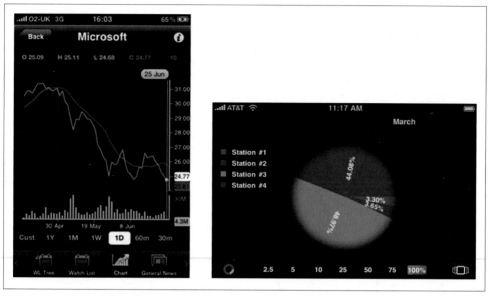

Figure 6-6. Blue Mobile and SmartGlance

The Android NewsWeather app and Daylight Calendar app uses date and times to filter the chart view.

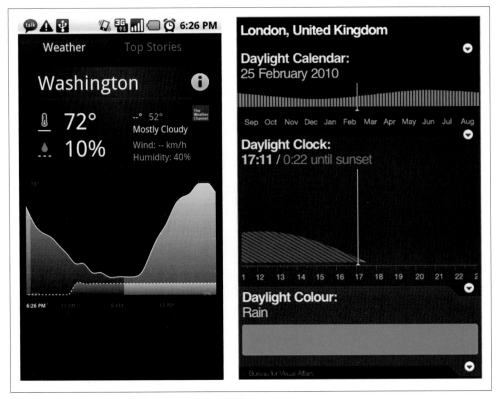

Figure 6-7. Android NewsWeather and DayLightCal

Filters can be applied to different aspects of the chart. This example from Sencha Touch Charts shows how a legend can be used to filter the data displayed. Tapping the icon slides out the legend. Tapping on "Coal" dynamically removes that variable from the chart about US Energy Consumption.

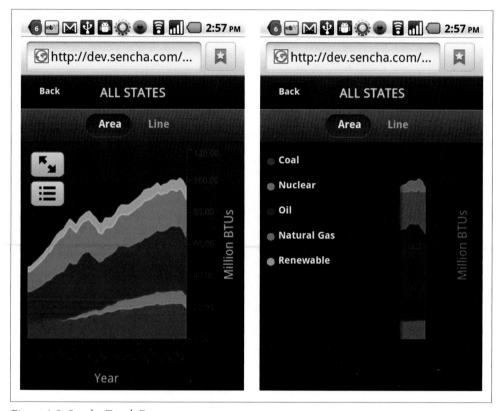

Figure 6-8. Sencha Touch Demo

 Use standard UI filter controls and patterns, see Chapter 4. Dynamically update the chart instead of using an "Apply" button.

Preview Window

This pattern is useful for communicating changes in data over time by providing more context and historical information than can fit nicely on a mobile screen without flicking.

Roambi offers handles for changing what is shown in the preview area. Once the "window" is set, it can be dragged (a rolling window), or the handles can be adjusted autonomously.

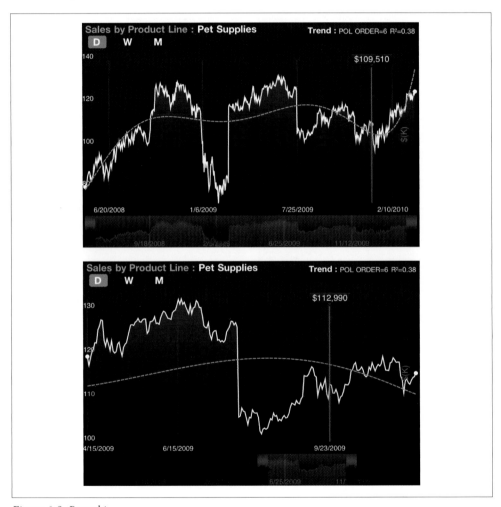

Figure 6-9. Roambi

Most financial applications use a read-only version of this pattern to show current numbers within the context of a longer period of time (i.e., the prices are up for today, but down for the month or year). More examples are in the Datapoint Details pattern.

Figure 6-10. Fidelity and Bloomberg

 The nature of the chart should determine if the preview window is read-only or interactive. If it is interactive, use large enough touch targets for easy manipulation.

Overview plus Data

This pattern is also covered in Chapter 3, but in this chapter it refers specifically to using a chart for the overview. Both of these examples use charts to summarize the most important information, and a table below with the detailed data.

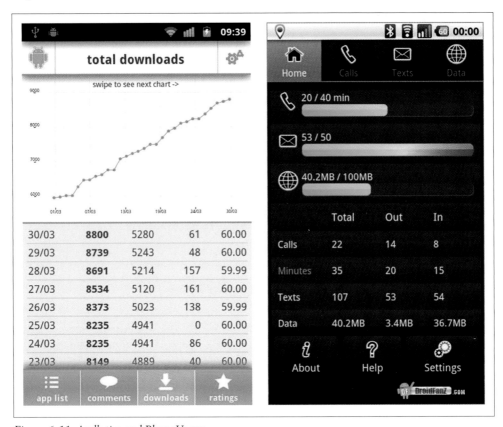

Figure 6-11. Andlytics and PhoneUsage

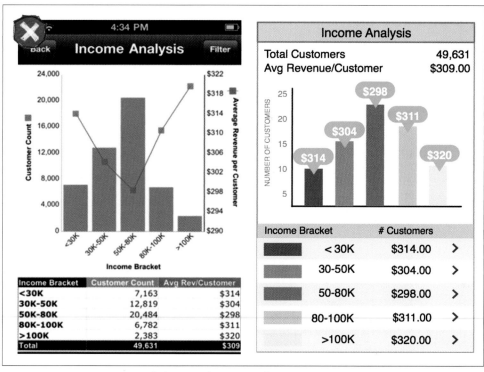

Figure 6-12. Microstrategy and alternate design (wireframe)

The overview should be simple and concise, and the table should be designed for an easy read. This example from MicroStrategy is cramped, and the font is smaller than the recommended size for mobile. The alternative is easy to read and summarizes the key metrics at the top of the screen: Total Customers and Average Revenue per Customer.

Test the chart to see if people can answer three simple questions: what is the topic, what is the important information, what are the values for the important information.

Datapoint Details

Since onHover doesn't exist in mobile, a different interaction is needed to show details for a data point. In this example, touching the chart will display details about the page views for the selected date.

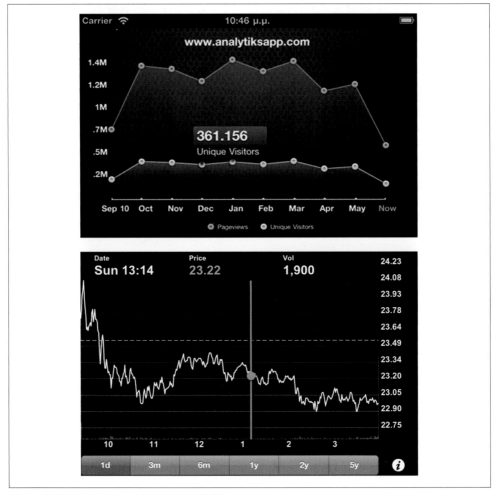

Figure 6-13. Analytiks and NASDAQ QMX

In this example from Yahoo! Finance, the data point is also highlighted in the preview window at the bottom of the chart.

Figure 6-14. Yahoo! Finance

Providing the details in proximity to the datapoint is preferable over using a modal dialog like this Sencha Touch example.

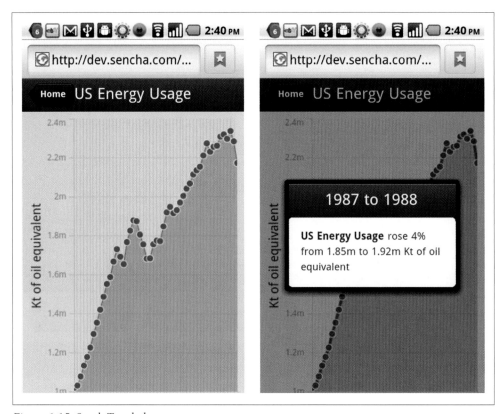

Figure 6-15. Sench Touch demo

Roambi offers a "detail mode" that can be accessed by tapping the + icon. The mode window or frame has a scrollbar for sliding to a certain datapoint. The folks at Roambi call this a "viewtron."

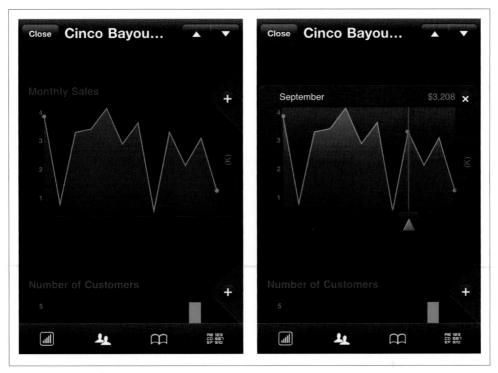

Figure 6-16. Roambi

 Charts on the Web have created an expectation for details to be displayed onHover. Consider implementing datapoint details onTap to provide the additional information users want.

Drill Down

Following the usability maxim "let there be input where there is output." It makes sense that a user will want to tap on the chart to drill down into the data. Drill Down and Datapoint Details can't co-exist, so determine which feature provides the most value and then select the appropriate pattern.

The Adobe Flex Sales Dashboard application my team designed uses Drill Down to show the data "behind" the bars in the first chart. Clearly show the drill down path as part of the page or chart title. In this example, we also kept the coloring consistent throughout the drilling. Depending on the OS, a back button in the UI may also be necessary.

Figure 6-17. Adobe Flex Sales Dashboard reference application

An invitation should also be included to encourage first time users to tap to drill down, see Chapter 8. Roambi displays help text with instructions to "Touch any bar to view data."

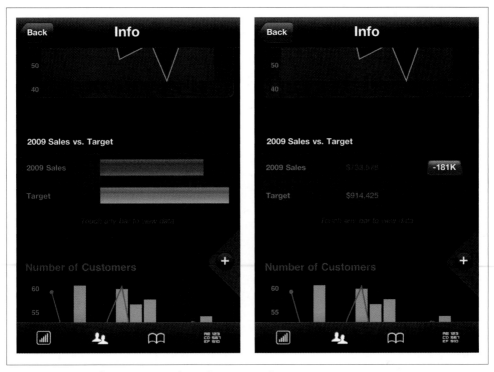

Figure 6-18. Roambi, invite to touch any bar to view data

 Invite the user drill down for more data. Use breadcrumbs to show the hierarchy.

Zoom

The chart might be only one of many elements on the screen, making it too small to read easily. It is common practice to invite the user to rotate their phone for a fullscreen, landscape view. The title and navigation elements are hidden to give the chart as much space as possible. Rotating the device back to portrait restores the navigation and other controls.

Figure 6-19. NASDAQ QMX

It is important to provide an invitation to rotate the device for the immersive chart view. NASDAQ QMX (above) uses a little illustration of a rotated phone, whereas Bloomberg (below) uses a label telling users to "Rotate to View Full Screen." This invitation is displayed only when the chart is tapped.

Figure 6-20. Bloomberg

Invite the user to rotate to landscape for a full screen view; automatically restore navigation when the device rotates back to portrait.

Pivot Table

Pivot tables, also referred to as *OLAP cubes*, are useful for creating unweighted cross tabulations. In desktop and web applications, the user can set up and change the summary structure by dragging and dropping graphically. This "rotation" or pivoting of the summary table gives the concept its name. [Wikipedia]

				Federal Shipping			Grand Total	
			unt	Count of Sales	Amount of Sales	Avg. Sale Amount	Count of Sales	Amount of
Venezuela			.43	31	$12,938.92	$417.38	118	$56,81
France			.25	52	$28,737.23	$552.64	184	$81,35
		Québec	.92	11	$6,052.15	$550.20	32	$28,87
Canada		BC	.39	28	$13,546.63	$483.81	43	$21,32
		Sub Total	.74	39	$19,598.78	$502.53	75	$50,19
Finland			.13	20	$4,889.84	$244.49	54	$18,81
Ireland			.49	18	$9,934.37	$551.91	55	$49,97
Portugal			.39	15	$5,438.49	$362.57	30	$11,47
Germany			.26	75	$53,474.88	$713.00	328	$230,28
USA			.03	103	$91,056.73	$884.05	352	$245,58
Denmark			.31	22	$18,295.30	$831.60	46	$32,66
		RJ	.37	11	$3,289.80	$299.07	83	$51,95
Brazil		SP	.40	32	$13,224.76	$413.27	120	$54,96
		Sub Total	.66	43	$16,514.56	$384.06	203	$106,92
Belgium			.56	23	$11,393.30	$495.36	56	$33,82
Switzerland			.39	20	$13,625.28	$681.26	52	$31,69
Austria			.77	37	$40,870.77	$1,104.62	125	$128,00

Figure 6-21. Viblend Pivot Table control for Microsoft Silverlight

Roambi has developed a simple interface for exploring data in a style similar to a pivotal table. The y-axis remains fixed; however, any dimension can be selected for the x-axis (see highlighted orange frame). For each dimension, a specific category can also be selected. This example shows how easy it is to explore the Year by Quarter Profit of All Cities, and then quickly refine the chart to just see this info for a specific Product Line: Books. With one more selection, the chart now shows information for All Cities, Books, via the Online Channel.

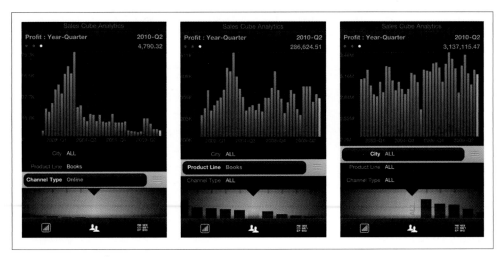

Figure 6-22. Roambi

 Keep the pivot table selection and resulting chart in a single screen. Apply the selections dynamically.

Sparklines

Sparklines, also called *microcharts*, are defined as an "information graphic characterized by its small size and high data density. Sparklines present trends and variations associated with some measurement, such as average temperature or stock market activity, in a simple and condensed way." [Wikipedia]

Sparklines are particularly well suited for mobile since they provide an overview of the shape or state of the data, but don't require the space of a full chart.

Figure 6-23. Analytix for Google Analytics and Norton Mobile Utilities

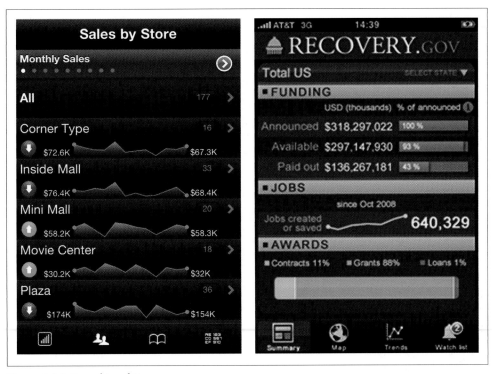

Figure 6-24. Roambi and Recovery.gov

 Follow sparkline design conventions. Validate the designs with your users. Consider combining Sparklines plus the Drill Down pattern to reveal the full chart details.

CHAPTER 7

Invitations

Patterns: Dialog, Tip, Tour, Demo, Transparency, 1st Time Through, Persistent, Discoverable

Do you remember the first time you used Photoshop? I remember opening the application and seeing a blank canvas and a vast array of powerful tools.

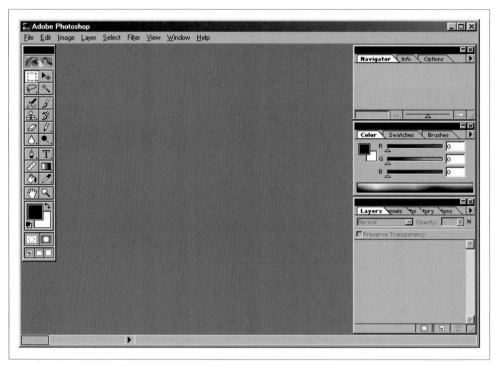

Figure 7-1. Photoshop 5.5

Well, I assumed the tools were powerful, but didn't know for sure. In fact, I didn't know how to get started at all. But I had quite a bit of money invested in the software and needed to learn it for work. So I bought *Sam's Teach Yourself Photoshop 5 in 24 Hours*, by Carla Rose and started learning.

Fast forward a decade or so. There are hundreds of thousands of mobile applications readily available in the marketplace. In any one category there are dozens of apps for the same purpose. Many of them are free, making it just as practical to download and try another app as it is to struggle for 5 minutes with an unintuitive interface.

Consider the initial experience with Layar Reality Browser, an augmented reality app.

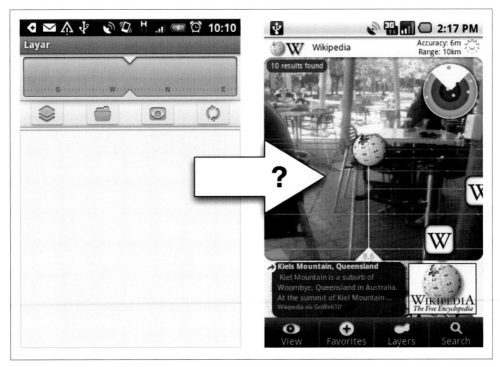

Figure 7-2. Layar Reality Browser

What would help me get from this gray screen to augmented reality? An invitation. Invitations are helpful tips that are displayed the first time a user opens an application or arrives at a new place. They suggest actions and guide the user to the intended functionality. A simple invitation can turn an otherwise discouraging first time experience into a satisfying one.

Mobile Invitation patterns include:

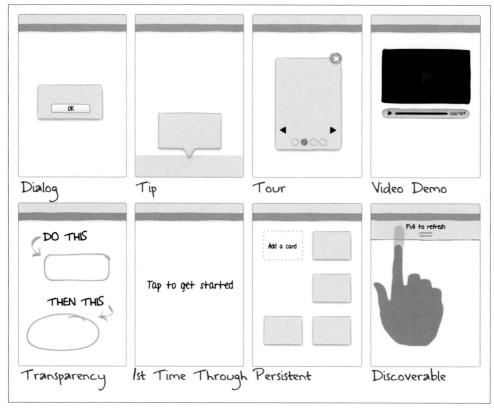

Figure 7-3. Patterns for Invitations

Dialog

A simple dialog with instructions is the most common type of invitation in mobile apps, probably because it is the easiest to program. It is also most likely to be dismissed and ignored.

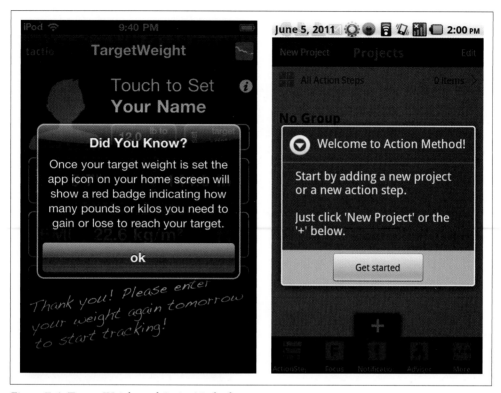

Figure 7-4. Target Weight and ActionMethod

 Keep dialog content short, and make sure there is an alternate way to access instructions from within the application.

Tip

A tip can be implemented anywhere in the screen, making it more contextually relevant than a dialog. And tips can be used on any screen, not just the home screen. In the eBay app, a tip is used to draw attention to the "save a search" feature, which could otherwise be overlooked since it is where the page title is normally displayed.

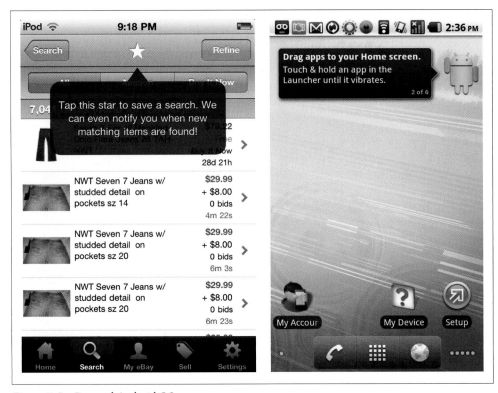

Figure 7-5. eBay and Android OS

ShoppingList reveals tips in each main section of their application.

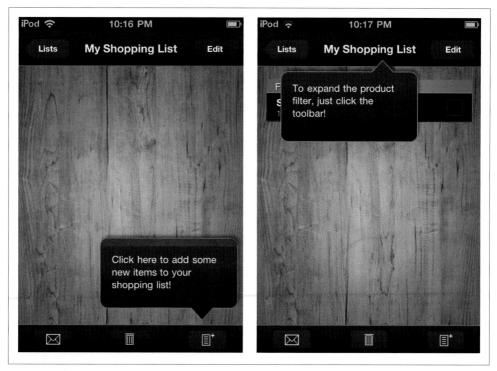

Figure 7-6. Shopping List

 Place tips in proximity to the feature they refer to, keep the content short, and remove the tip once interaction begins (i.e., when the screen is touched).

Tour

A tour provides the ultimate invitation by offering a screen-by-screen, feature-by-feature exploration of the application. The Nike GPS tour is an excellent example of this pattern. The tour is optimized for mobile with concise copy, vivid graphics, simple navigation, and a clearly marked exit. The Tour is offered on the home screen, and once launched you can tap through each of the seven tips. Nike and CalcBot use page *indicators*, Apple's term for the little dots, to indicate the current step in the tour.

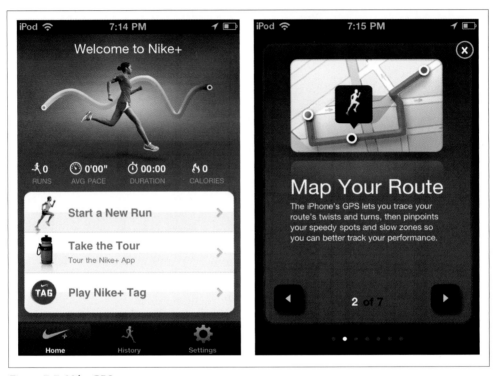

Figure 7-7. Nike GPS

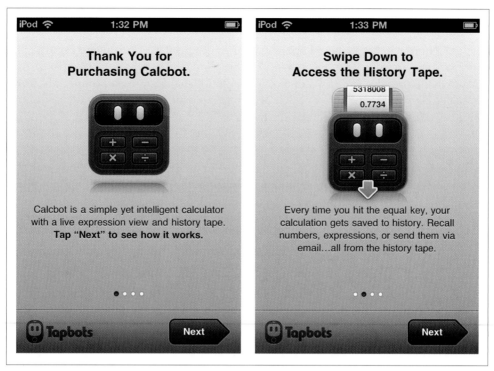

Figure 7-8. CalcBot

 A tour should highlight key features of the application, preferably from a (user) goal perspective. Keep it short and visually engaging.

Video Demo

A video demo may be the best form of invitation for applications that rely on specific actions/interactions since it demonstrates the application in action. Roambi uses a custom demo to showcase its wide selection of data visualizations and the use of certain gestures for optimal navigation and exploration. Google Goggles has a demo in their tour that can be opened and viewed in YouTube.

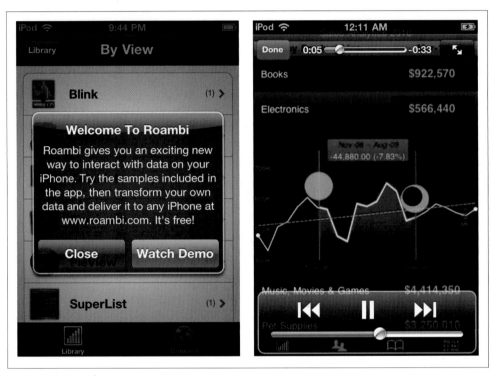

Figure 7-9. Roambi

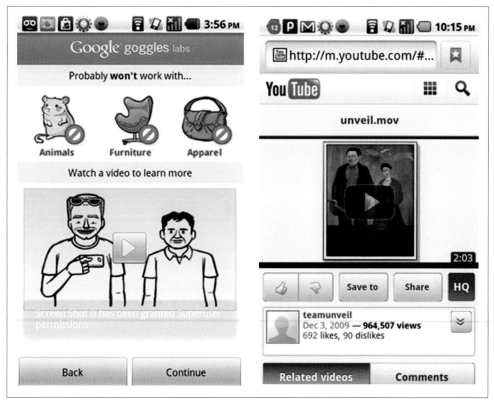

Figure 7-10. Google Goggles

 Demos should showcase key features or show how to use the application from a standard workflow perspective. Common video features (stop, pause, volume controls...) should be provided.

Transparency

While the rest of these patterns exist on the Web, the transparency is unique to touchscreen devices (so far). Typically seen on home screens, a transparency is a see-through layer with a usage diagram positioned over the actual screen content. Pulse and Phoster both use this invitation pattern to quickly and visually explain how to navigate content in the apps.

Figure 7-11. Pulse and Phoster

 Transparencies should be used judiciously and are not meant to compensate for poor screen designs. Remove the transparency once interaction begins (i.e., when the screen is touched).

1st Time Through

Unlike the other invitations, 1st Time Through invitations don't precede the screen they refer to. 1st Time Through invitations are built into the screen design. They remain in the interface until they are overwritten with content or the action is performed. Many note taking apps, like Mini Diary and PageOnce, use 1st Time Through invitations to immediately engage the user to add content.

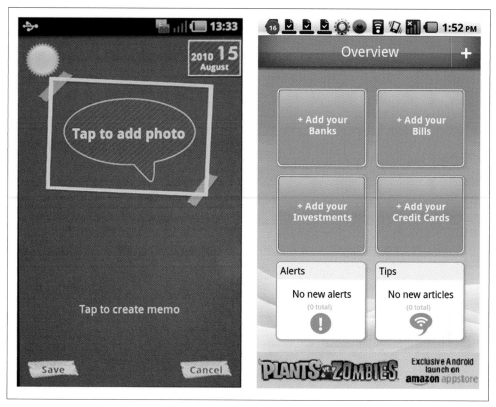

Figure 7-12. Mini Diary and PageOnce

 Clearly differentiate the invitation from other content with images or other visual cues (i.e., don't use the same color and size text for the invitation as is used for regular content).

Persistent

Persistent invitations are built into the screen and remain visible. This example from Jamie Oliver Recipes suggests switching to landscape mode to uncover an additional feature. Whether this is your first time on this screen, or 10th time, the prompt is still displayed. Spring Pad uses an embedded, persistent invitation to show that more notes can be added by tapping on the "+".

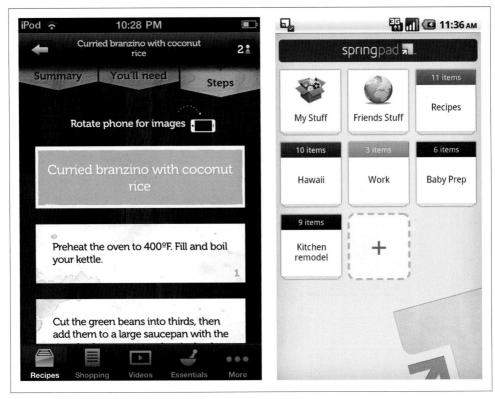

Figure 7-13. Jamie Oliver Recipes and Spring Pad

 Keep it short. Clearly differentiate the invitation from other content with images or other visual cues (i.e., don't use the same color and size text for the invitation as is used for regular content).

Discoverable

A discoverable invitation might seem like an oxymoron, but it is an effective way to encourage specific interactions without cluttering the screen. These invitations are meant to be discovered when performing a common gesture, like flicking or swiping.

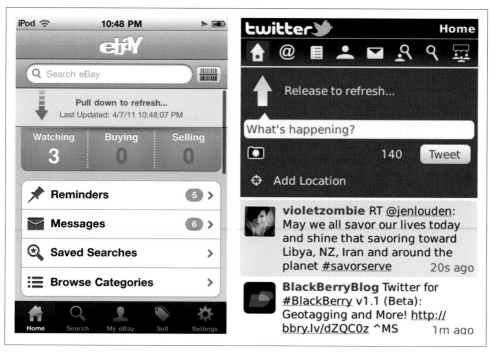

Figure 7-14. eBay and Twitter

 Use Discoverable invitations sparingly. The most common instance of this pattern is for prompting a data refresh.

Feedback Patterns: Errors, Confirmation, System Status

Affordance Patterns: Tap, Flick, Drag

Feedback

The usability principle of feedback states "Provide appropriate, clear, and timely feedback to the user so that he sees the results of his actions and knows what is going on with the system." Feedback can vary from simple progress indicators and confirmation messages, to more sophisticated animations and effects. Mobile feedback patterns include:

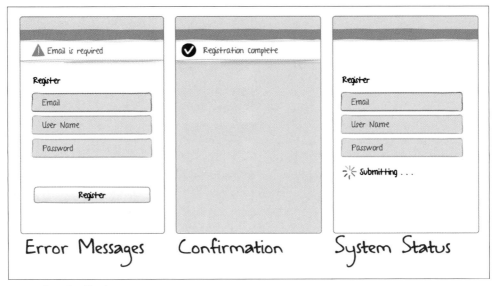

Figure 8-1. Feedback patterns

Error Messages

Error messages should be expressed in plain language (no codes), precisely indicate the problem, and constructively suggest a solution. Highly visible error messages on the screen, like TaxCaster and Mint, are preferable to a modal dialog, since a dialog may cover up the issue.

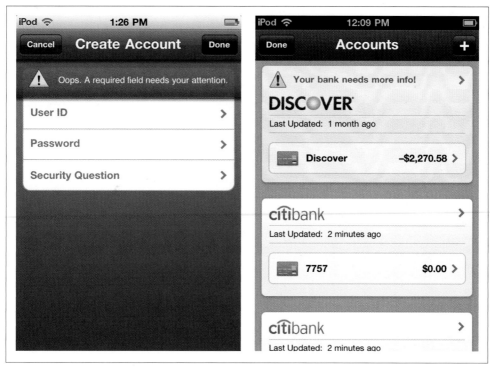

Figure 8-2. TaxCaster and Mint

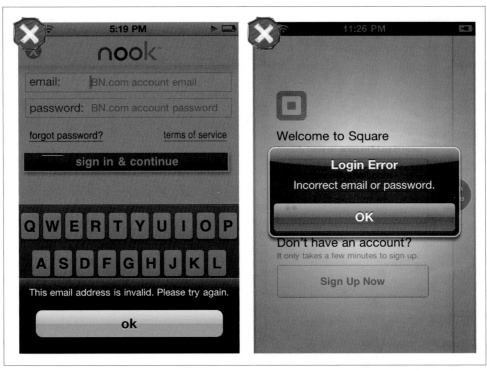

Figure 8-3. Barnes & Noble Nook, error message in Action Sheet; Square, error message in dialog

 Use plain language that offers a solution for resolving the issue. Make the error visible; use in-screen messaging instead of modal dialogs.

Confirmation

Confirmation should be provided when an action is taken. But avoid the Idiot Box anti-pattern (see Chapter 10), and instead look for a way to provide feedback without disrupting the user flow.

For example, Whole Foods and Sprout both use animation to show when an item has been added to a list. Upon tapping the add button, the item "falls" into the list object on the tab bar.

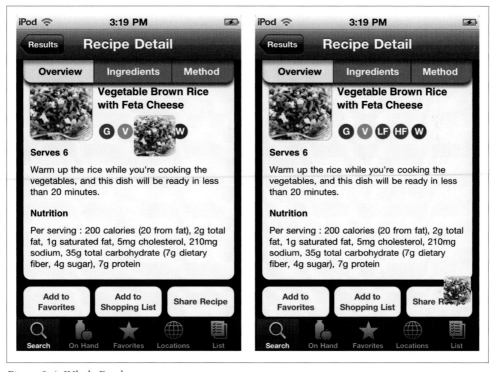

Figure 8-4. Whole Foods

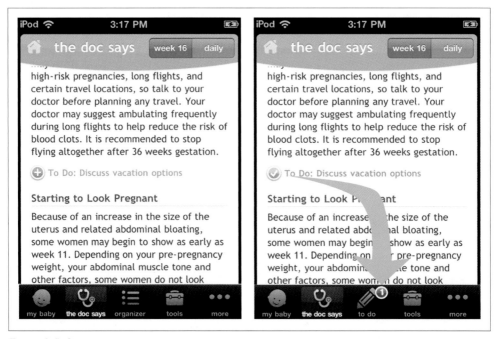

Figure 8-5. Sprout

Inline feedback as seen in Kik, and State Changing buttons as seen in the Android Marketplace, are other unobtrusive ways to provide confirmation without interrupting the flow.

Figure 8-6. kik

Figure 8-7. Android Marketplace

Sometimes confirmation messages need to be prominently displayed, like at the end of a transaction or when information is submitted.

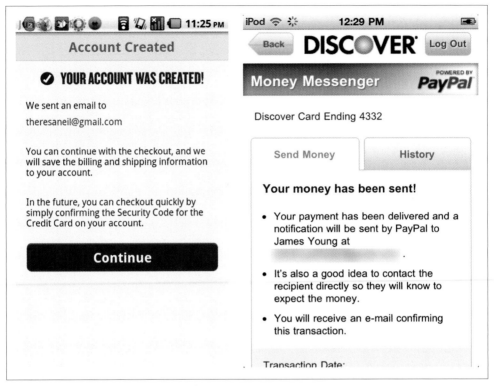

Figure 8-8. Best Buy and Discover card

 Provide confirmation when an action is taken, but don't break the user's flow to do so.

System Status

Timely feedback increases users' confidence with an application. Netflix shows that they are "Loading your queue…" instead of leaving one to wonder if the app is frozen. System Status can be portrayed with a simple message, and animated indicator, a loading bar, or combination of elements. The status can be integrated in the page like Netflix, Android Marketplace, and PageOnce, or in an overlay like TaxCaster.

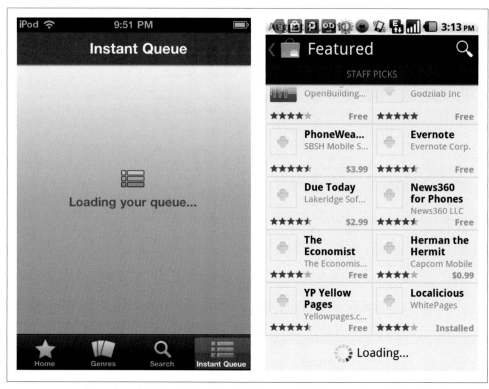

Figure 8-9. Netflix and Android Marketplace

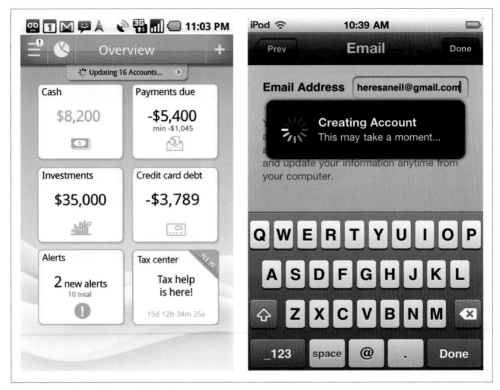

Figure 8-10. PageOnce and TaxCaster

Kayak uses a progress bar to show the status of flight results. Notice the different treatment in the iOS application and the Android application.

Figure 8-11. Kayak on Android and on iOS

For potentially lengthy processes, offer a cancel button, like the SXSW app does for downloading the new schedule. The Adidas miCoach app offers a warning upfront about the file size, but should offer a cancel option as well.

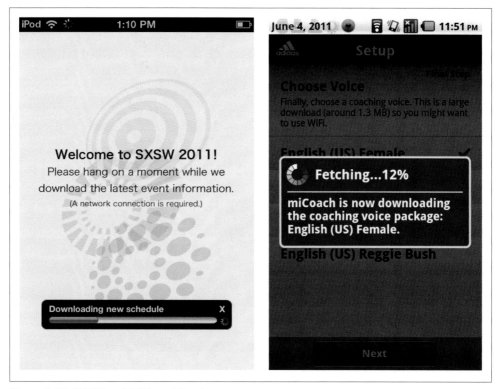

Figure 8-12. SXSW and Adidas miCoach

 Provide feedback about the system's status. Offer a cancel option for potentially lengthy operations.

Affordance

Affordance is the quality of an object that allows an individual to perform an action, like a handle on a drawer or knob on a door. Common examples in software include: drag handles, page peels, 3D controls like buttons and sliders.

Mobile applications can leverage the same patterns. Here are a few common patterns found on touchscreen UIs:

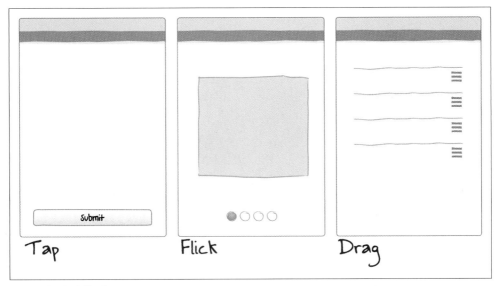

Figure 8-13. Affordance patterns

Tap

Visual design techniques like beveling and shadows can make elements appear tappable. Pictory and GroupMe both use these effects to make it readily apparent which controls can be tapped.

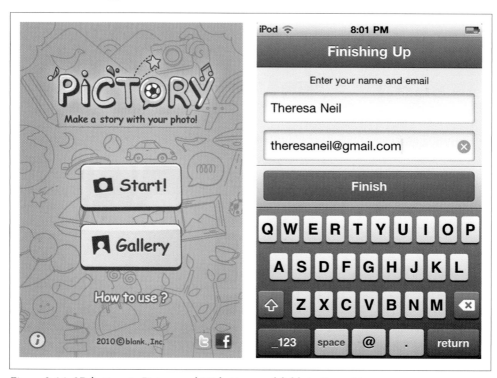

Figure 8-14. 3D buttons in Pictory and 3D buttons and fields in GroupMe

It is important to apply this effect properly though. Yelp's search button doesn't look like a button, whereas every element in this form looks like a button, even the field labels.

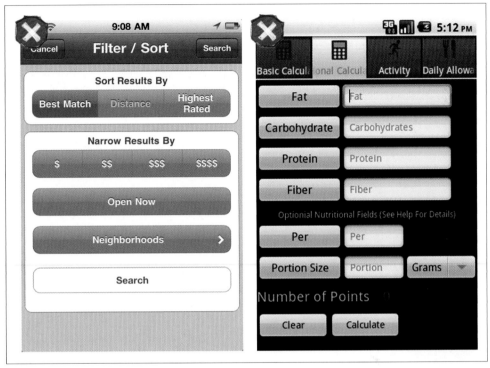

Figure 8-15. (Left) Yelp's search button doesn't look tappable; (Right) all of these labels look tappable

 Use common visual design techniques to indicate tappable controls. But apply 3D effects judiciously; extra shadows and bevels can decrease readability.

Flick

There are many ways to provide affordance that there are more things to view. The iOS page indicator control, those little dots, has been widely adopted across web and mobile apps alike.

Figure 8-16. FreeTime and Audible

Another option is to show a little bit of the next item at the edge of the screen, either the bottom or on the side. Both of these techniques encourage the user to flick the screen to see more.

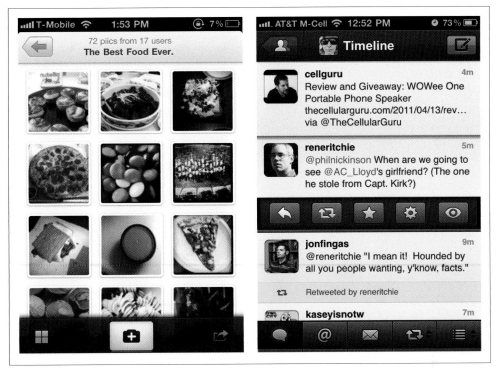

Figure 8-17. Piictu and TweetBot

A less common option is to show a scrollbar. The bar may also act as a touch target for quickly jumping to a certain spot. Roambi uses an almost transparent scroll bar on the right with a green dot to indicate the current spot. Skype uses the alphabet scroll bar, a control commonly found in iOS apps.

Figure 8-18. Roambi's Cardex and Skype

 Use a page indicator or show the edge of the next item to provide affordance that flicking will reveal more items. Avoid heavy weight scroll bars.

Drag

Drag handles indicate that an item can be moved, rearranged, or reordered. They work well on items in a list like in Yahoo Finance and Roambi.

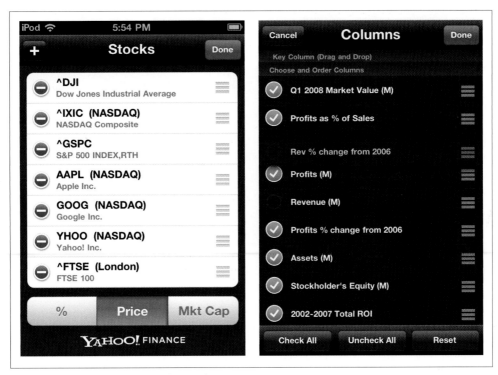

Figure 8-19. Yahoo! Finance and Roambi

Sliders also rely on drag handles, as do preview windows, see Chapter 6.

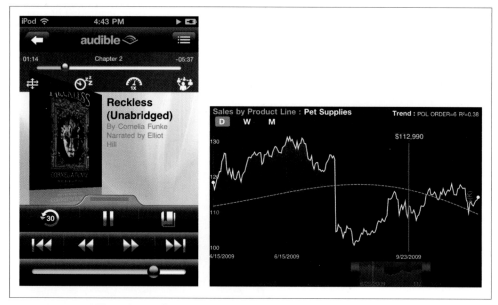

Figure 8-20. Audible and Roambi

 Use a recognizable icon for the handle. Consider using an invitation along with the drag handle to let users know this feature is available.

CHAPTER 9

Help

Patterns: How To, Cheat Sheet, Tour

Mobile applications should be easy to learn and quick to master. But no matter how intuitive the application may be, some form of Help should be provided. A couple of common Help patterns are:

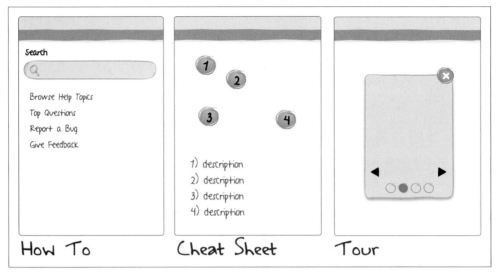

Figure 9-1. Help Patterns

How To

How To's are just simple explanations of how to use the app. They can be one page like Phoster and Pictory or part of a larger help system like Awesome Note.

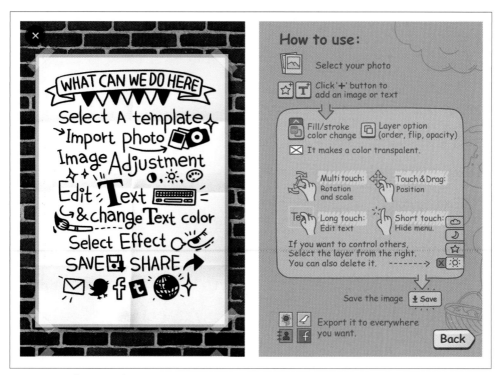

Figure 9-2. Phoster and Pictory

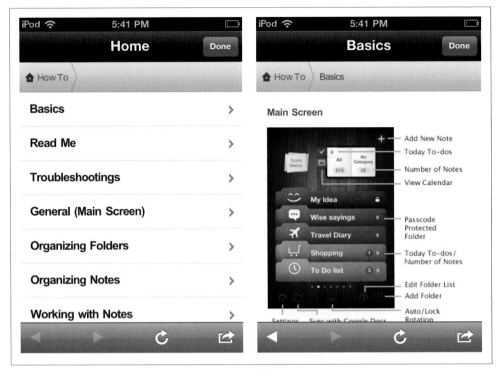

Figure 9-3. Awesome Note

 Use a combination of screenshots, illustrations, and text to communicate in a How To.

Cheat Sheet

A Cheat Sheet offers a light weight way to introduce all the elements on the screen. Tap'n'scratch uses a separate page for this, whereas Android Swype opted for a dialog, see Chapter 7.

Figure 9-4. Swype on Android and Tap'n'Scrap

 A Cheat Sheet is no substitute for good design, but it can help users get comfortable and productive with the application.

Tour

A Tour is probably the best solution for providing help within the application. It can be offered at first use and should be accessible at any time in the future. More information and examples of Tours are in Chapter 7.

Figure 9-5. TripIt and FreeTime

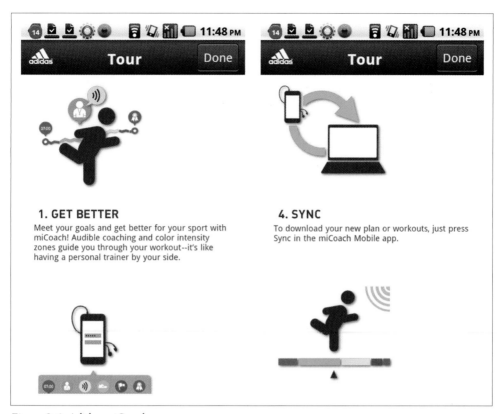

Figure 9-6. Adidas miCoach

Although Valspar's Quick Start Guide is attractive and full of great content, it might not be so quick; there are +12 pages to swipe through. Try to keep a Tour down to a half dozen pages.

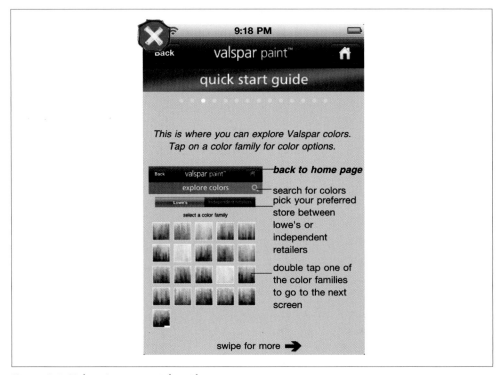

Figure 9-7. Valspar's not so quick guide

 The Tour should highlight key features of the application, preferably from a (user) goal perspective. Keep it short and visually engaging.

CHAPTER 10

Anti-Patterns

Anti-Patterns: Novel Notions, Metaphor Mismatch, Idiot Boxes, Chart Junk, Oceans of Buttons

What are anti-patterns? Wikipedia defines them as:

> Anti-patterns, also called pitfalls, are classes of commonly-reinvented bad solutions to problems. They are studied as a category so they can be avoided in the future, and so instances of them may be recognized when investigating non-working systems. The term originates in computer science, apparently inspired by the Gang of Four's book Design Patterns, which displayed examples of high-quality programming methods.
>
> —Wikipedia, Anti-Pattern.

Like the software anti-pattern counterparts, the following design anti-patterns are common pitfalls to avoid.

Novel Notions Anti-Pattern

Novel designs are intended to be new, edgy, creative, and innovative. But most of the time they're just bad, hard to understand, and harder to use. Richard Gunther, creator of the BUI* Gallery, explains it as: "You can usually tell when a mobile app development team comes from an old web development background. They often attempt to translate old user interaction models to the new platform and assert their "creativity" by introducing non-standard UI elements."

Novel Notions can be found anywhere in an application, from primary navigation down to an individual control, interaction, or gesture. Weight Watcher's has a number of Novel Notions in their application, the most obvious being their primary navigation. They created a custom menu drawer that contains a Springboard.

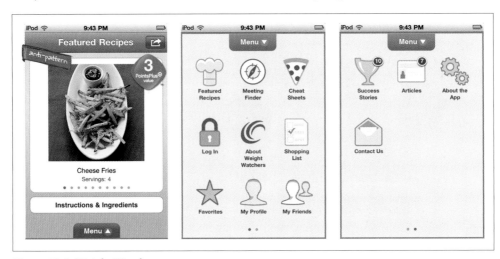

Figure 10-1. Weight Watchers

This is just terrible. It is clunky to use, the organization is random, and important features for converting visitors to paying customers are essentially hidden (in the second page of the Springboard). I can see what Weight Watchers wanted to achieve here, but the application would be easier to learn and navigate if they had used a standard navigation pattern and organized the menu options.

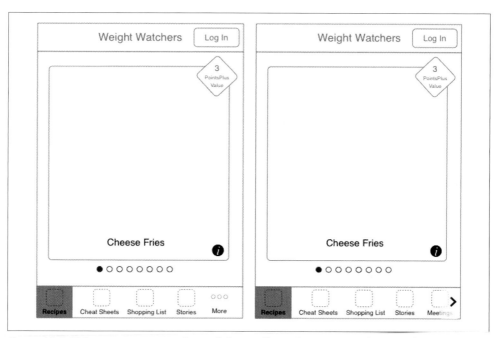

Figure 10-2. Tab menu option, wireframe (left); scrolling tab option, wireframe (right)

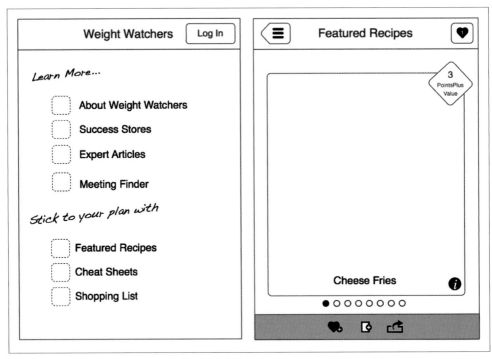

Figure 10-3. List menu option, wireframe (left); interior screen concept (right)

The Fly Delta iPhone had a similarly "novel" menu, but they have since replaced it with another Novel Notion, a discoverable (onFlick) footer with a Home button and a link to "Contact Us."

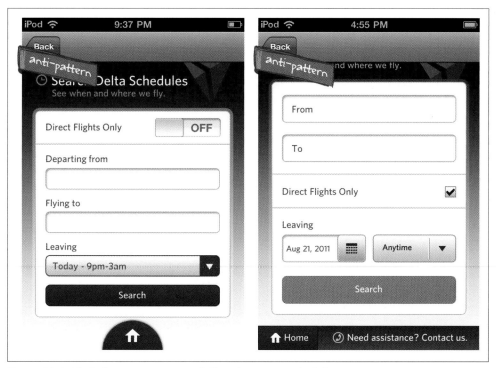

Figure 10-4. Fly Delta, previous menu (left) and new menu (right)

If it was important to offer one-click access to the main page, the standard iOS tabs would work just fine. "Contact us" would be better positioned in the top right than in a hidden footer. Does this menu design make the application innovative? No, just a little harder to use.

Sometimes a talented and experienced design team can pull off a Novel Notion with enough finesse to make it usable. Gowalla's designers took a standard Tab menu and flipped it over making a beautiful and usable menu. Forecast tried to imitate the Gowalla menu without understanding the nuances of the design.

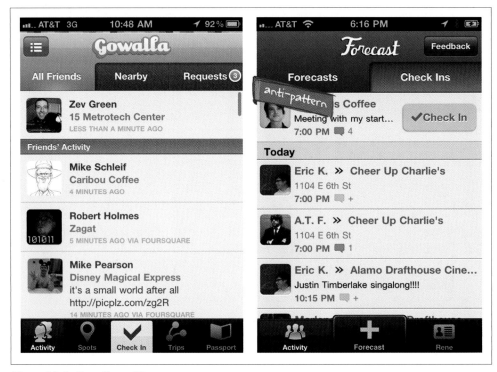

Figure 10-5. Gowalla and Forecast

With only two stylized tabs in Forecast, it takes a little longer to figure out, am I looking at Forecasts or Check Ins? The visual design doesn't help; the recessed design of the Check Ins tab make it appear selected when it's not.

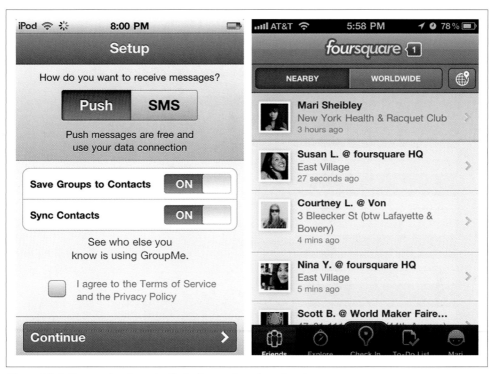

Figure 10-6. Recessed style typically indicates the selected option

A simple toggle bar would alleviate this confusion. Actually, after looking at the flow of this application more closely, I think a single activity feed showing forecasts and check ins combined sorted by time would be the best option. This design relies on Forecast establishing a recognizable "forecast" icon for indicating if friends have forecast a place or checked in to a place.

Figure 10-7. Wireframe with iOS standard tabs

Forecast also designed a custom tab bar, but it too lacks polish. This type of custom bar works well for applications with one main call to action, like posting to Pinterest and sharing with Instagram. Forecast really has two main actions, Forecast then Check In.

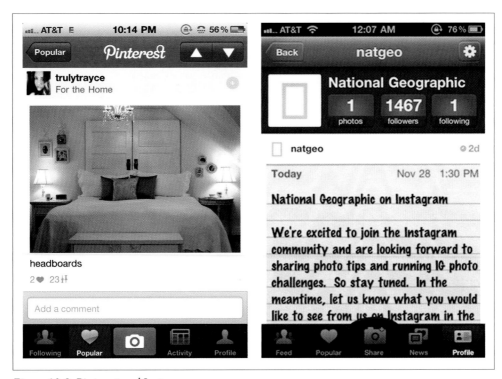

Figure 10-8. Pinterest and Instagram

A persistent *Add Forecast* button would probably work just as well, with an invitation for new users to help with their first time through. If not, an icon for Forecast should be developed and used for the custom toolbar.

Figure 10-9. Add Forecast button with invitation (left); alternate version with a custom toolbar (right)

 If you are looking for a way to innovate with your application, focus on your core features and offerings, but rely on best practices for the interface design. If you design a custom control, rigorously test it and refine it to make sure it is usable.

Metaphor Mismatch Anti-Pattern

This anti-pattern is a result of picking the wrong metaphor for the interface. Metaphor Mismatch can occur at a low level, when a control or icon is used inappropriately, or at a high level, where the conceptual model for the application doesn't match the user's mental model.

Control Mismatch

A simple example of this anti-pattern at a low level is in the app Calorific, where they offer a list of every age instead of a date picker. Another example is in Easy Point Calculator, where all the labels are styled to look like buttons.

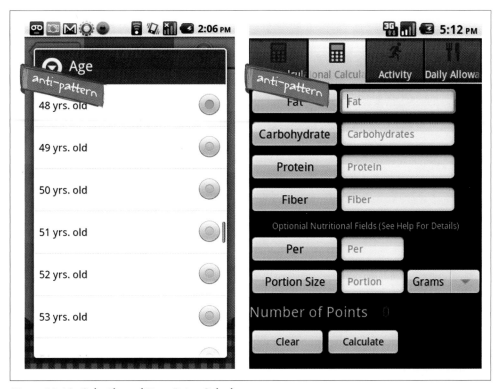

Figure 10-10. Calorific and Easy Point Calculator

What To Expect's Baby Tracker also has a Metaphor Mismatch between the controls used for navigation and the ones people expect to find. On first glance, WTE seems to have four baby tracking options and a View Log button.

Figure 10-11. WTE's Baby Tracker

But there is a full menu of options wedged in the pink filter below the title bar. Although this filter control works well for navigating content in apps like ACL and 360News, it is a poor choice for *primary navigation*.

Figure 10-12. ACL, filter control for shows; news360, filter control for stories

Anecdotal evidence: I installed the What To Expect app when my son was 3 weeks old. I only saw the four tracking options on the springboard, and none of the other features, so I deleted the app.

Icon Mismatch

Icons are another contender for the Metaphor Mismatch anti-pattern. People expect familiar icons to offer specific features. Using a familiar icon in an unfamiliar way will cause confusion.

In the top right of the Weight Watcher's app there is the iOSsendButton. It normally offers options like Send email, Send to Facebook. I was surprised to see Favorites and Add to Shopping List options listed here. Offering a standard toolbar would make this application more intuitive, and probably result in higher adoption of the "favorite" and "shopping list" features.

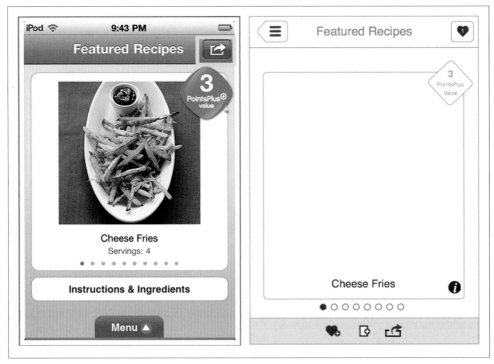

Figure 10-13. Send button has unexpected options

Mental Model Mismatch

One of my favorite examples of this anti-pattern was in a trouble ticket system my previous employer rolled out. When we had a technical issue, from a forgotten password to a dead laptop, we had to sign into the system, browse the list of issues, select an issue, then add it to a shopping cart and checkout. Great design for a retail shopping app, total mismatch for a technical support application!

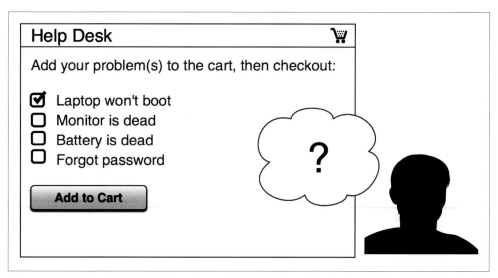

Figure 10-14. Help desk example

Take this example from the ABC News iPad app. A globe for navigating news content? Oh, well that makes sense perhaps if stories are surfaced from specific geographic locations. But they are not. In fact the ABC News globe has nothing to do with "the globe." It is just a spinning sphere that is hard to read and harder to browse.

Compare it with the globe used in GeoWalk, an educational application for exploring facts from around the globe. GeoWalk has fact cards placed at different locations on the globe, so you can explore facts for a specific region.

Figure 10-15. ABC News and GeoWalk

 Metaphors, from iconography and controls to conceptual models, can be used to enhance an experience. Using them improperly will make the application hard to learn and use.

Idiot Box

In Alan Cooper's About Face 3 book he describes this scenario:

> A person enters a highly productive mental state by working in harmony with her tools....Interrupting a user's flow for no good reason is stopping the proceedings with idiocy and is one of the most disruptive forms of excise.

Bill Scott built on this concept of "stopping the proceedings with idiocy", and coined the Idiot Box anti-pattern. My favorite Idiot Box is in Photobucket's registration form. After I painstakingly complete 10 fields and click a big green button labeled "I Agree, Sign Me Up!", this dialog pops up.

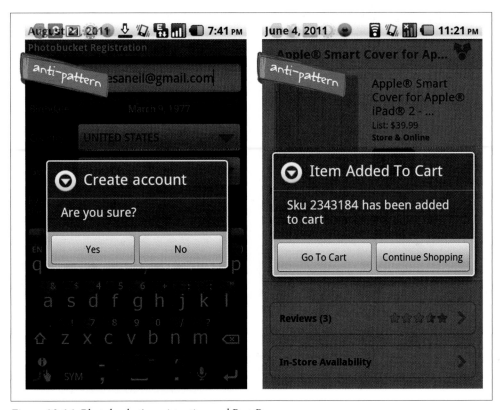

Figure 10-16. Photobucket's registration and Best Buy

Uh, yeah. I'm sure I want to create an account, that would be why I filled in all the fields and tapped the big green button.

Best Buy relies on Idiot Boxes to provide feedback that an item has been added to the shopping cart. A less disruptive, and more effective technique for this is to simply increment the number of items in the cart. Zappos even goes a step farther and uses a transition to show the item being added to the cart, accomplishing two goals at once:

- providing feedback the item has been added
- showing the customer where the cart is accessed in the app.

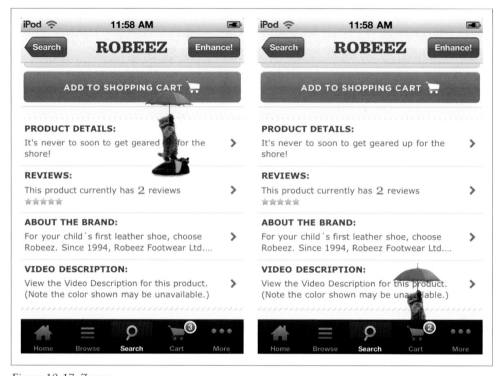

Figure 10-17. Zappos

You do not need to show a cat with an umbrella to provide adequate feedback. See Chapter 8, for more ideas.

 Avoid disrupting the workflow, only show a confirmation dialog when an irreparable action is being taken (like a permanent delete).

Chart Junk

Edward Tufte coined the term *Chart Junk* in his 1983 book *The Visual Display of Quantitative Information*, in reference to charts like these:

Figure 10-18. Chart junk or infographic?

I personally consider this to be a decent infographic, not Chart Junk. But I can get behind the anti-pattern of Chart Junk as "all the visual elements in charts and graphs that are not necessary to comprehend the information represented on the graph, or that distract the viewer from this information." [Wikipedia]

In this anti-pattern example from Brain Challenge (below), the design of the chart, from the double gradient columns, to the high gloss, beveled, shadowed, iconic buttons as labels, distracts more than it enhances the data. The next example from SmartGlance is almost illegible with its green felt table with rolling red dice in the background.

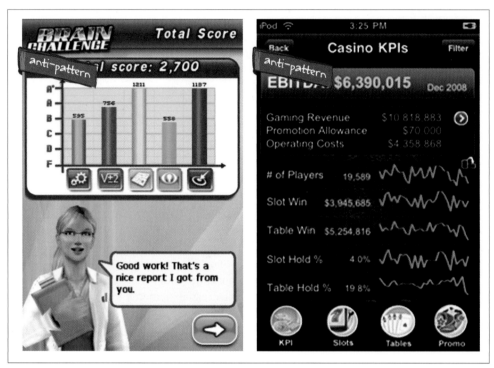

Figure 10-19. Brain Challenge and SmartGlance

QlikView's reports module contains a couple of anti-patterns; metaphor mismatch for filtering and icons, novel notions for report selection, and chart junk. Roughly half the screen is used for an image carousel of possible charts (and their reflections). The rest of the screen is devoted to big, colorful 3D charts with illegible labels.

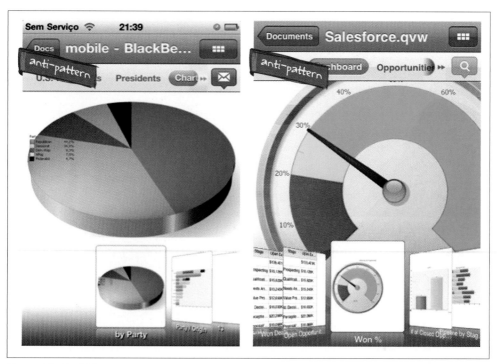

Figure 10-20. QlikView

But just because your chart is beautiful, doesn't mean it is in the clear. Chart Junk often poses as eye candy, and gets added to make the charts "sexier." For instance, in this analytics app, does the curved line reflect an average or a threshold? Nope, it's just part of the background. Compare this with Gerald Nunn's OnTrack app, which uses different colors to indicate which data are in and out of the normal range.

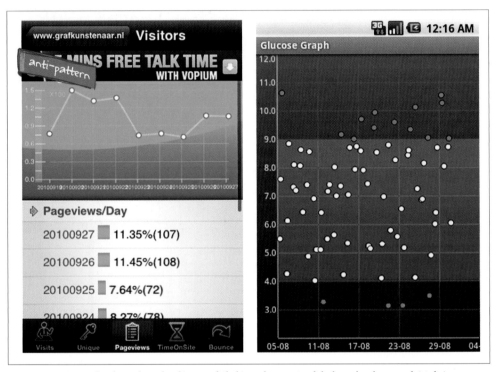

Figure 10-21. Misleading chart background (left) and meaningful chart background (right)

WeatherPro has gorgeous charts, but they would be easier to read without the:

- alternating gradients in each column
- redundant y-axis labels
- hour increments

Shortening the day labels (Mon, Tue, Wed, etc.), would allow for larger, easier to read font. Oh, and a legend would help too. Upon further investigation, it turns out the "*i*" icon, will reveal the legend. Ideally, the legend would be displayed by default with an option to hide it, see Chapter 6.

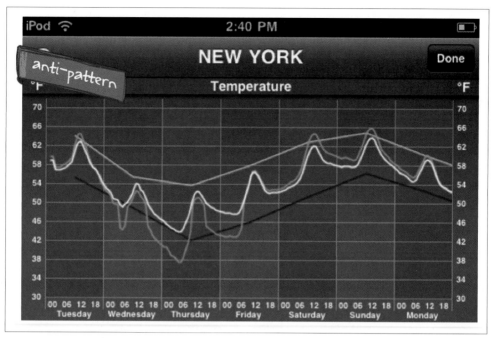

Figure 10-22. WeatherPro

While playing with WeatherPro, I stumbled upon another Metaphor Mismatch. To share a chart, you pull down the screen, a gesture that is normally used for refreshing data. See how their customers feel about that design decision:

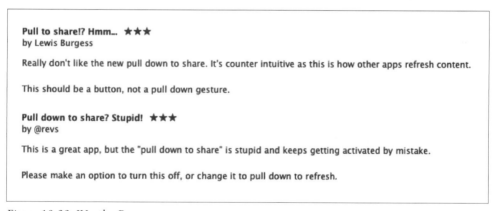

Figure 10-23. WeatherPro

Only use visual elements in charts and graphs that are necessary to communicate the information represented on the graph.

Oceans of Buttons

Bill Scott and I first named this anti-pattern while conducting usability reviews at Sabre Airline Solutions in 2002. We tasked our team with evaluating dozens of web and desktop applications to find the ones most in need of a UI redesign. Many of the applications were Java Swing or Visual Basic, and had a button bar either down the right or across the bottom. Sometimes there would be more buttons than could fit horizontally, so two rows were displayed. All the buttons were the same size and same color, basically the same visual weight, so it was difficult to determine which one to click without reading all of them.

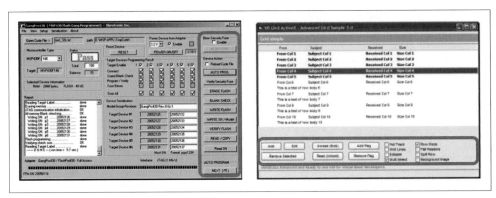

Figure 10-24. Oceans of buttons in Visual Basic and Java desktop applications

eBay's Android app suffers from Oceans of Buttons; however, their iPhone app uses the Dashboard pattern, which is a good solution for this anti-pattern.

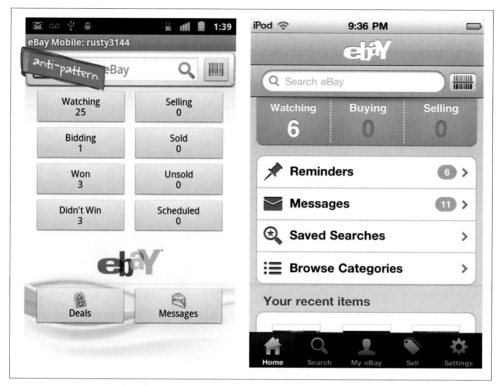

Figure 10-25. eBay Android, oceans of buttons; eBay iOS, no ocean

Footfeed (below) shows every option for every activity in the feed. 1Mobile shows the same button on every table in the row. Contextual tools are a better choice when you find yourself repeating the same buttons for every row in a list or table, Chapter 5.

Figure 10-26. Footfeed and 1Mobile Market: Replace repeating buttons with contextual tools

At first glance, Pushbi appears to have a standard action bar, but in reality, it is just an Ocean of Buttons. Navigation buttons are intermingled with action buttons (Home, Back, Chart, Settings, Share). Even more buttons, presumably only applicable to this one chart, are displayed up top. VisualKPI has a similar problem, but their ocean floats above the chart.

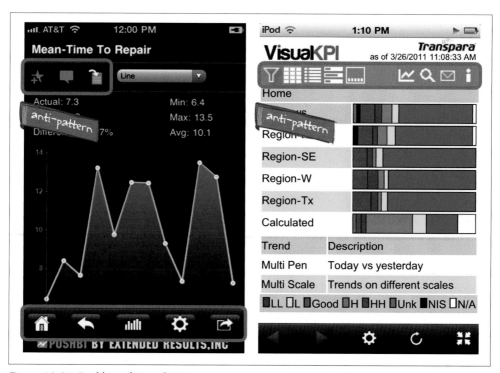

Figure 10-27. Pushbi and VisualKPI

 Use standard patterns for displaying page level actions. Provide contextual tools for item level actions instead of repeating the same button. Keep page level actions visually separate from navigational elements.

Additional Resources

Companion website and blog at www.mobiledesignpatterngallery.com (*http://www .mobiledesignpatterngallery.com*).

Checkout the **flickr** photostream (*http://www.flickr.com/photos/mobiledesignpattern gallery/collections/*) for more examples of each pattern.

For expert mobile design tips, follow me on 🐦 @mobilepatterns (*http://twitter.com/ mobilpatterns*).

Navigation

Primary Navigation

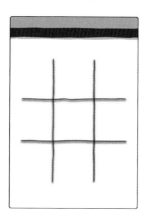

Springboard

Use a grid layout for items of equal importance, or an irregular layout to emphasize some items more than others. Consider personalization and customization options.

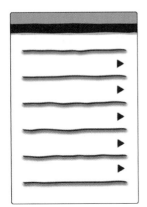

List Menu

List Menus work well for long titles or those that require sub text. Applications using List Menus should offer an option on all internal screens for returning to the List Menu, usually a button in the title bar with a list icon or the word "menu."

Tabs

Clearly indicate the selected menu item by visually differentiating the selected tab from the others. Use easy to recognize icons or icons with labels.

Gallery

The Gallery pattern works best for frequently updated content that people want to browse.

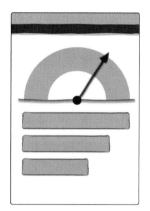

Dashboard

Don't overload the dashboard; conduct research to determine the key metrics to include.

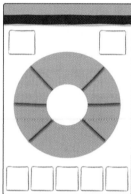

Metaphor

Use the Metaphor pattern judiciously, as a poorly implemented metaphor can look a lot like the Novel Notion anti-pattern in Chapter 10.

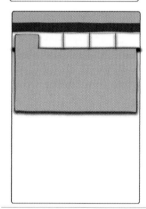

Mega Menu

Determine your information architecture before choosing the navigation pattern. Choose a more appropriate pattern, like Tabs, if there are only a few major sections in the app.

Secondary Navigation

Page Carousel

The page carousel works best for navigating a small number of pages. Use a visual indicator to reflect the number of screens, and current screen. Flick is the common gesture to navigate the carousel.

Image Carousel

The Image Carousel works best for displaying fresh visual content, like articles, products, and photos. Provide visual affordance, either with arrows, partial images, or page indicators (dots) that more content can be accessed.

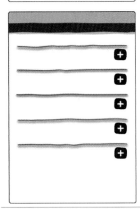

Expanding List

The Expanding List pattern works best for progressively disclosing more details or options for an object.

Forms

Sign In

Don't innovate on the sign in screen, use best practices to make it easy for users to get signed in. Provide a way to retrieve a forgotten password.

Registration

Keep it short, preferably one screen, with the Register button above the fold. Make it simple for an already registered use to sign in.

Checkout

Design for speed, efficiency, and reassurance. Eliminate unnecessary fields and minimize the number of pages and steps.

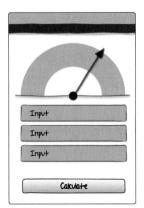

Calculate

Use standard form conventions for design and layout. If possible, visualize the results in the same page.

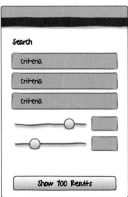

Search Criteria

Avoid overwhelming the user with options; aim for a single page of criteria. Use appropriate controls that are finger friendly and fast.

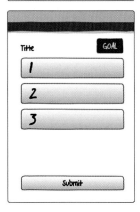

Multi-Step

Show the user where they are and where they can go. Eliminate unnecessary fields and minimize the number of pages and steps.

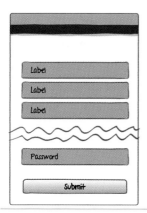

Long Form

Don't artificially break the form into steps just to prevent scrolling. Do ruthlessly edit the form for any unnecessary fields. Follow OS standards for button placement.

Tables

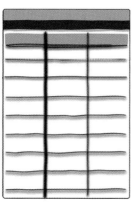

Table with Header

Avoid using dark gridlines and vertical dividers. Left align text and right align numbers. Don't overload the screen. Consider an alternate pattern if there is too much information to fit on a single screen.

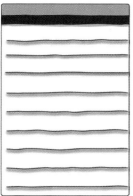

Headerless Table

Three rows of information maximum per fat row. Use smaller and/or lighter font for less important details. Don't guess what the most important information is, ask your customers and validate the designs.

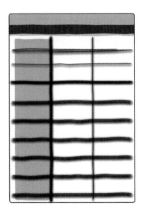

Fixed Column

Provide visual affordance which column is fixed, and that swiping can reveal more data.

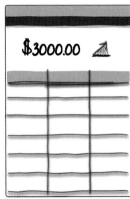

Overview plus Data

The Overview should be presented above the Data and be easy to understand at a glance.

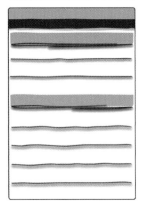

Grouped Rows

Visually differentiate the summary rows from the other rows in the table.

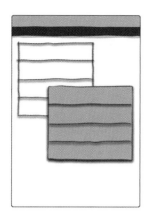

Cascading List

Use a fairly flat information hierarchy to avoid deep drilling (more than 3 levels) in the application. Deep drilling may not be avoidable if the Cascading List pattern is used to navigate a user defined information hierarchy.

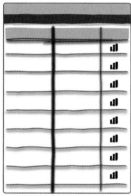

Table with Visual Indicators

Choose visual indicators that are immediately recognizable; avoid gratuitous icon use.

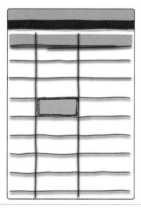

Editable Table

Leverage web and desktop design best practices for editable tables. Avoid using editable tables for bulk data entry, or when extensive amounts of edits could be necessary.

Search

Explicit Search

Offer a clear button in the field and an option to cancel the search. Use feedback to show the search is being performed (Chapter 8, Feedback & Affordance).

Search with Auto-complete

Show feedback if there could be a delay in displaying the results. Consider emphasizing the matching search text in the search results.

Dynamic Search

Works well for constrained data sets, like an address book or personal media library, but may be impractical for searching huge data sets.

Scoped Search

Offer reasonable scoping options based on the data set. Three to six scoping options are plenty; consider a search form for advanced searching capabilities.

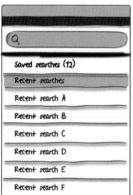

Saved and Recent Searches

Saved searches typically require additional steps for naming a search for reference later, whereas recent searches are implicitly saved and surfaced. Consider which one will best serve your users' needs.

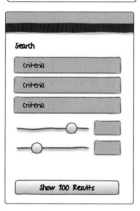

Search Form

Minimize the number of input fields. Implement OS specific input controls properly. Follow form design best practices (alignment, labels, size), see Chapter 2.

Search Results/View Results

Label the results with the number returned. Use live scroll instead of paging. Apply a reasonable default sort order.

Sort Patterns

Onscreen Sort

Clearly show which option is selected or "on." Consider the Sort Order Selector pattern if the option labels don't fit nicely in a toggle button bar.

Sort Order Selector

Follow OS design conventions for choosing the selector control, or choose an OS neutral interface control. Clearly show which sort option is applied.

Sort Form

Consider a lightweight sort option toggle or sort order selector patterns before choosing this pattern.

Filter

Onscreen Filter

Filter options should be clearly worded and easy to understand. Show the filters that are applied or "on." Don't use this filter pattern for navigation, see Chapter 10, Metaphor Mismatch.

Filter Drawer

Keep the options list short, avoid scrolling. Consider a Filter Form for lengthier or multi-select filter options. See Chapter 6, Charts with Filters for examples on filtering chart data.

Filter Dialog

Keep the options list short, avoid scrolling. Consider a Filter Form for lengthier or multi-select filter options. See Chapter 6, Charts with Filters for examples on filtering chart data.

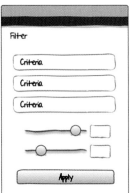

Filter Form

Don't over-design the filter, a simple onscreen filter or drawer will usually suffice. If a Filter Form is necessary, follow form design best practices.

Tools

Toolbar

Toolbars are generally displayed at the bottom of the screen and contain screen level actions. Choose icons that are familiar and easy to recognize, or use labels plus icons.

Option Menu

Choose direct interactions when possible. Don't hide navigation in the Option Menu. Consider the Call to Action Button pattern if you have a single action for the screen.

Call to Action Button

Don't hide the main call to action in a menu or disguise it as an unrecognizable icon in a toolbar. Make it obvious (good contrast) and spell it out (clear label).

Contextual Tools

Choose direct interactions when possible. If buttons are necessary, they should be displayed in proximity to the actionable object. Choose a familiar icon or use a text label.

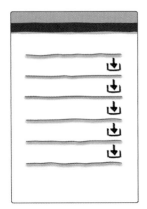

Inline Actions

Choose direct interactions when possible. Inline Actions should be in proximity to the actionable object. Choose a familiar icon or use a text label. Max one to two Inline Actions per object.

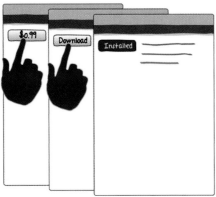

Multi-State Button

Multi-State Buttons work well for a series of tightly correlated actions that will to be performed in succession with limited screen real-estate.

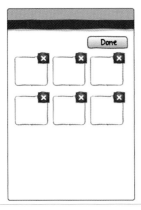

Bulk Actions

Bulk actions like delete and reorder are best handled in an edit mode. Provide an obvious option for exiting the mode.

Charts

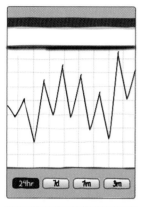

Charts with Filters

Use standard UI filter controls and patterns, see Chapter 4. Dynamically update the chart instead of using an "Apply" button.

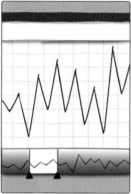

Preview Window

The nature of the chart should determine if the preview window is read-only or interactive. If it is interactive, use large enough touch targets for easy manipulation.

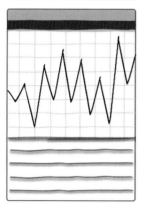

Overview plus Data

Test the chart to see if people can answer three simple questions: what is the topic, what is the important information, what are the values for the important information.

Datapoint Details

Charts on the Web have created an expectation for details to be displayed onHover. Consider implementing Datapoint Details onTap to provide the additional information users want.

Drill Down

Invite the user drill down for more data. Use breadcrumbs to show the hierarchy.

Zoom

Invite the user to rotate to landscape for a full screen view; automatically restore navigation when the device rotates back to portrait.

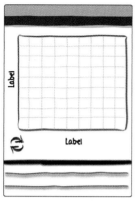

Pivot Table

Keep the pivot table selection and resulting chart in a single screen. Apply the selections dynamically.

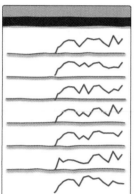

Sparklines

Follow sparkline design conventions. Validate the designs with your users. Consider combining Sparklines plus the Drill Down pattern to reveal the full chart details.

Invitations

Dialog

Keep dialog content short, and make sure there is an alternate way to access instructions from within the application.

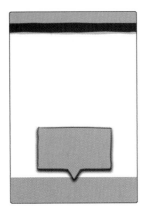

Tip

Place tips in proximity to the feature they refer to, keep the content short, and remove the tip once interaction begins (i.e., when the screen is touched).

Tour

A tour should highlight key features of the application, preferably from a (user) goal perspective. Keep it short and visually engaging.

Video Demo

Demos should showcase key features or show how to use the application from a standard workflow perspective. Common video features (stop, pause, volume controls, etc,...) should be provided.

Transparency

Transparencies should be used judiciously, and are not meant to compensate for poor screen designs. Remove the Transparency once interaction begins (i.e., when the screen is touched).

1st Time Through

Clearly differentiate the invitation from other content with images or other visual cues (i.e., don't use the same color and size text for the invitation as is used for regular content).

Persistent

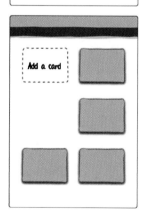

Keep it short. Clearly differentiate the invitation from other content with images or other visual cues (i.e., don't use the same color and size text for the invitation as is used for regular content).

Discoverable

Use Discoverable invitations sparingly. The most common instance of this pattern is for prompting a data refresh.

Feedback

Error Messages

Use plain language that offers a solution for resolving the issue. Make the error visible; use in-screen messaging instead of modal dialogs.

Confirmation

Provide confirmation when an action is taken, but don't break the user's flow to do so. See Chapter 10, Idiot Boxes.

System Status

Provide feedback about the system's status. Offer a cancel option for potentially lengthy operations.

Affordance

Tap

Use common visual design techniques to indicate tappable controls. But apply 3D effects judiciously, extra shadows and bevels can decrease readability.

Flick

Use a page indicator or show the edge of the next item to provide affordance that flicking will reveal more items. Avoid heavy weight scroll bars.

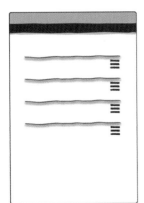

Drag

Use a recognizable icon for the handle. Consider using an invitation along with the drag handle to let users know this feature is available.

Help

How To

Use a combination of screenshots, illustrations, and text to communicate in a How To.

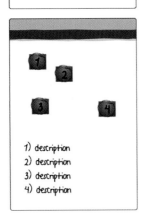

Cheat Sheet

A Cheat Sheet is no substitute for good design, but it can help users get comfortable and productive with the application.

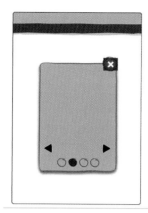

Tour

A Tour should highlight key features of the application, preferably from a (user) goal perspective. Keep it short and visually engaging.

About the Author

Theresa Neil works as a user experience consultant in Austin, Texas. Her small team of seasoned UX designers and developers work closely with clients to create applications that make people happy, productive, and confident. Her newest project is a tablet application for restaurants that will allow customers to order from their table. Check out other projects on her site, www.theresaneil.com (*http://www.theresaneil.com*), and follow her on Twitter @theresaneil (*http://twitter.com/theresaneil*).